IT'S SIMON

THE STORY OF THE DUBLIN SIMON COMMUNITY

Ursula Coleman

THE GLENDALE PRESS

First published in Ireland by
The Glendale Press Ltd
1 Summerhill Parade
Sandycove
Co. Dublin, Ireland

British Cataloguing in Publication Data
Coleman, Ursula
It's Simon: the story of the Dublin Simon Community
1. Dublin. Welfare services for homeless persons.
Dublin Simon Community, history.
I. Title
362. 5′8′0941835

ISBN 0 907606 41 5

Typeset by Wendy A. Commins, The Curragh, Co. Kildare
Make-up by Paul Bray Studio
Printed in Great Britain by Southampton Book Company.

This Book is Dedicated
to the Memory of
Ian Hart
1939–1980

Ian Hart

CONTENTS

ACKNOWLEDGEMENTS

When it comes to thanking those who have helped me to write this book, I am faced with a difficult task. I cannot name them all. The 1983/4 members of the Dublin Simon Community were very helpful; they gave me their time and made available to me any documentation I needed. I spoke also with many former members, some of whom I have quoted liberally in the text.

The residents with whom I spoke were helpful and trusting. Their names, with one exception, have been altered in the text in order to protect their privacy. It was John Joe Higgins' wish, however, that his real name be used.

Without Mary Cleary and her typing staff in the Economic and Social Research Institute it would have been difficult for me to present a decent manuscript to the publisher. Brian Harvey, formerly of the National Simon Office, acted as my editor/adviser. His advice and encouragement were invaluable. Finally I would like to thank Tom Turley of Glendale Press for the interest he took in the project.

PREFACE

DR IAN HART

An Appreciation

Ian Hart's death in March 1980 at the age of forty, deprived the Irish social research community of one of its most creative and committed talents. Ian was one of the most prolific and enterprising members of that community, pioneering Irish research in a number of fields but particularly adolescent development and juvenile delinquency. But the loss goes far deeper. More than any other individual, Ian successfully bridged the gap between those who investigate and those who act or have an impact on policy-making; and at a personal level, his warmth, humanity and good humour make for a sorely missed colleague, both professional and personal, even a decade after his death.

Educated in Cork – receiving his BA, MA and PhD, all in psychology, from University College, Cork – Ian joined the staff of the Economic and Social Research Institute in 1967. The diversity of his research work in thirteen years at the Institute is well represented in the following selection of articles he published in *The Economic and Social Review* – the main social research journal published in Ireland.

'A survey of some delinquent boys in the Irish industrial school and reformatory' Volume 1, No. 2.

'Inter-generational social mobility and individual differences among Dubliners' (with B. O'Sullivan) Volume 2, No. 1.

'Empirical classifications of types among delinquent referrals to a child guidance clinic' (with P. McQuaid) Volume 4, No. 2.

'Absenteeism at National Schools – educational and social aspects' Volume 6, No. 3.

Numerous other articles appeared on these and other topics in such journals as *Administration*, *Journal of Child Psychology and Psychiatry*, *Irish Journal of Psychology*, *Contemporary Psychology*, and *Pulse*.

In these writings, the topic of criminology predominates. Through his articles and particularly through his ESRI research paper, *Factors Relating to Reconviction Among Young Dublin Probationers*, Ian firmly established criminology as a social science discipline in Ireland.

From the start, Ian's research interests were paralleled by a desire to do something about the problems he studied, to move beyond dispassionate research and toward a more humane, more active and more effective response. Despite his substantial work-load, his initial involvement with the Simon Community as a clinical psychologist was the starting point for Ian's ten-year association with the organisation, including active membership in the Dublin Simon Community committee. His experiences with Simon were recounted in two remarkable publications, *A Group Approach to Socially Deprived People* (with D. McMahon, published by The Runa Press) and *Dublin Simon Community 1971-1976: An Exploration* (ESRI Broadsheet No. 15). Anyone who knew Ian will recognise in these documents his acute, often self-mocking sense of humour, his perseverence in the face of difficulties, his deep humanity, and his energy. Both are models for the blending of social science research with intervention.

It is a paradox that reformers of society in general can often be indifferent to the particular. Not so Ian; he could never lose sight of the individuals that formed his research data, and in both his public and private life he practised what he preached.

The range and number of Ian's activities is formidable indeed: CARE, HOPE, Dublin Simon Community, the Jervis Street Hospital drug unit, the Task Force on Child Care Services, Trudder House Juvenile Itinerant Project and the Association for Deprived Children are but examples of the groups to which he gave of his time and experience. Ian's busy schedule left little opportunity to meet his colleagues informally. However, we all remember his deep and rich sense of humour and the laughter in which his head would rear back, a laugh that eased tension and reduced problems to their proper proportion. Ian always had time for someone who wanted to discuss a problem; many people did, and if the problems were not always solved, Ian invariably provided insight and perspective.

It has been an inspiration to his research colleagues, and especially to those of us at the ESRI, that one so committed to reform opted for social research as his chief means of achieving it. There is always a danger that a passionate concern with human suffering may impair the objectivity of research. Few have been so aware of the danger as Ian himself, and few have countered it so successfully. Characteristically, he sought to articulate the problem, to understand its ramifications, and to take all possible precautions against it. His many research publications provide testimony to his success.

Contemporary staff and Council members at the ESRI partly funded the book on the story of the Dublin Simon Community, to commemorate Ian. Both the book itself and the work it describes and commemorates provide a fitting tribute to one at once so disciplined and so committed.

INTRODUCTION

The reality of homelessness may never have touched you personally. You may never even have spoken to anyone who is genuinely homeless. But homelessness is a reality in Irish society today. 1987 was designated *International Year of Shelter for the Homeless.* At a seminar held in January 1987 to mark the opening of the special year, it was estimated that there were between three and five thousand homeless people in Ireland. Many become homeless as a result of economic pressures. Unemployment, low Social Welfare payments and eviction are contributory factors. Homeless people are ordinary people who fall on hard times. The longer they remain homeless, the less ordinary they feel. Unless they can manage to return quickly to a settled way of life they are in danger of becoming permanently homeless.

The Simon Community is a voluntary organisation which has been working with the single homeless in Ireland since 1969. It attempts to provide shelter, food, clothing and above all companionship for men and women, over the age of forty, who are unable to provide themselves with accommodation. Some people simply use the Simon Community as an emergency service; for others it has provided a more permanent 'home'. Simon Communities now exist in Dublin, Cork, Dundalk, and Galway. There is also a National Simon Community Office, based in Dublin.

The Dublin Simon Community has been in existence since 1969. It began as a student-type organisation which tried to highlight the plight of the homeless. Throughout the seventies and eighties it has developed the services it now provides and has stabilised at an organisational level. Like any voluntary organisation, it has had its strengths and its weaknesses, its triumphs and its failures. This book, for which the research was carried out during 1983 and 1984, attempts to document the story of the first fifteen years of the Dublin Simon Community.

The story of the early years is told in the first two chapters.

Thereafter the approach is thematic although the chronological thread is held throughout. Selecting themes for consideration proved a daunting task in view of the volume of documentary material available on the activities of Dublin Simon. Inevitably, therefore, this cannot claim to be a comprehensive history of the organisation. Although particular aspects of Simon policy are explored in some detail, the aim of this book has been to provide an account of Dublin Simon which would be of interest to the general reader as much as to the Simon Community member.

Certain aspects of the Dublin Simon Community experience have already been documented. *A Group Approach to Socially Deprived People* (Runa, Dublin, 1975), co-authored by Ian Hart and Dermot McMahon, describes the effects of group psychotherapy on the residents of one Dublin Simon Community house. *Dublin Simon Community 1971-1976: An Exploration* (ESRI, Dublin, 1978) is an account by Ian Hart of his involvement with the Community during the stated period. It is written from the research psychologist's point of view. *Seal Le Síomón* (An Clóchomhar, Dublin, 1984) gives a lively personal account of the characters and events which made an impression on the author, Jack Ryan, during his years as a voluntary worker with the Community.

It is perhaps fitting that this book should be published in 1990, the year in which Dublin Simon celebrates its coming of age. The Community has of course changed and developed since 1984. Many would see the opening of the purpose-built Night Shelter at Usher's Island in 1989 as a high point – a moment of victory. The 1988 'Artist in Residence' scheme, which was funded by the Arts Council, was a creative development. It involved an artist, who was based in Sean McDermott Street, working with ten residents who subsequently exhibited and sold their work at a Temple Bar gallery. On a sadder note, Frank O'Leary's death in July 1989 left a great emptiness in the hearts of his many friends. Other deaths too, all too many in recent years, have allowed the note of sadness to creep into Simon life. But during these years the organisation has continued to mature: organisational structures have been developed in order to ensure maximum participation in decision-making; projects have been evaluated systematically and effective referral is considered crucial; relationships with other agencies, both voluntary and statutory, have been developed and nurtured; and Dublin Simon is now keen to seek greater statutory funding for its projects.

The homeless people who have become part of Dublin Simon over the years have contributed enormously to all those who have worked with the Community; they have taught us the basic facts about homelessness – what causes it, what the reality is like, and where the possible solutions might lie. Many of them have shown extraordinary courage and good humour in the face of circumstances which would have defeated other people. This story is, above all, their story; without them there would have been no Dublin Simon Community.

PROLOGUE

Dublin 1983 . . . taking the initiative

When I asked the late Frank O'Leary, chairman of the Dublin Simon Community, what was distinctive about Simon, he thought for a few moments and answered:

'It takes the initiative, goes out to meet people rather than waiting for them to come. Take Miriam for example, she keeps after people, sees them again and again, until they realise that she is not a threat.'

I went out with Miriam one Sunday in January, when the trees in St Stephen's Green were bare and the sky was overcast. Outside the University Church she brought the car to a sudden stop; observant as always, she had noticed one of her 'clients' shuffling along the footpath, head down, coat wrapped tightly around him in an effort to cheat the wind. She pulled two pound notes from her bag and shoved them at me.

'Give those to him, stick them into his pocket if necessary,' she ordered me.

I obeyed and was rewarded by a shy smile from the old man.

'I haven't seen him for ages,' Miriam told me as we drove towards the quays. 'He usually stays up around Ranelagh, and the soup-run visits him, but he hasn't been there since before Christmas. He looks in bad shape and could do with a few bob. We'll look out for him in Ranelagh later on.'

As we passed by Usher's Island, Miriam pointed out a large warehouse which, she told me, was for sale. Dublin Simon were trying to raise the money to purchase it; they desperately needed a new night shelter. The houses in Sarsfield Quay, across the Liffey, which were currently being used as a shelter, had been condemned in the early seventies. A new shelter had been a priority for years, but finding a suitable premises had proved extremely difficult.

A middle-aged married woman with a grown-up family, Miriam has an imposing appearance. She is tall and stately, with jet-black hair swept back from a face which is full of character. As we drove on towards the Liberties to collect a member of her follow-up team, she talked about the needs of Simon residents.

'Should we not be providing them with rooms of their own?' she wondered. 'A bit of privacy and comfort, but some communal facilities and back-up service as well. Our people have a right to housing. Maybe we should be pressurising the Health Board to provide suitable accommodation.'

Miriam thinks about all of this incessantly. She is a real 'Simon' person. Her interest does not remain with any one project but extends itself to all who are homeless or friendless. She finds 'new' people; she keeps in touch with those who leave to go to prison or hospital or flats. She has been involved in Simon since the early seventies and has influenced its policy on many issues. Miriam is a 'doer' rather than a talker; an Executive Committee member, she does not enjoy that side of Simon. Her real commitment is to relationships with social outcasts and, as she says herself:

'My problem is that, if I make a relationship with someone, it doesn't stop there.'

It was approaching midday when we collected Pat Normanly, a younger woman, who worked closely with Miriam. We headed for Ringsend, stopping along the way to buy two large bags of coal. Our first visit was to Mrs Burke, an oldish battered-looking woman, who was living in an open shed at the back of the Port and Docks Board office, facing out onto the dump at Ringsend. She had been there for three years. A heavy drinker, she can be dangerous and offensive when under the influence. When Miriam had last visited her on Christmas Eve she had got a poor reception. She had no idea how things would be this time. She parked the car in such a way that it would be possible to make a quick getaway. This was not necessary. Mrs Burke was in good form, delighted to see us and pleased to get the coal and some food. She offered to pay but Miriam would have none of it. There was a mattress and a few odds and ends in the shed, which had been bare when Simon had been contacted several months before by an employee of the Port and Docks Board. Mrs Burke's only means of cooking was a small smoky fire burning just outside the shed. In rainy weather she lights it inside and lets the smoke blow out.

On a corner of the dump, only five minutes away from Mrs Burke's, Marty lives in a neat little garden hut. Nearby there is a foundation for a building, a little concrete room which will be built soon to replace the hut. Marty talks to Miriam, he trusts her. Otherwise he is reticent. A middle-aged man, he seems happy with his lot. He has an old bicycle with no tyres, which he uses to wheel around the bits of scrap he collects on the dump. No-one seems to know whether he actually sells anything or not. On a cold day you might see him playing hurling on a green patch in Ringsend. He needs to keep warm and sometimes his uniform – a cap, a large coat tied around the waist, and boots – does not suffice.

Marty's life has improved greatly since Miriam arrived on the scene. He used to live in a makeshift house of tin and cardboard. He was afraid to speak to the soup-runners, who came at night. He had nobody to rely on. He did not trust Miriam at first either. But after she brought him his food daily during a bout of illness, they became friends. Miriam has applied for housing for him; in the meantime she is determined that he shall be as comfortable as possible.

Next we drove along Merrion Road and turned right up a little laneway between Blackrock College and a large private demesne, which had recently been sold to property developers. At the end of the laneway stood another garden hut. This one was equipped with a comfortable bed, blankets and some shelving. But 'The Dreamer' wasn't there. We found him in an old shed on Kelly's land. Miriam explained that he had lived there for many years. While the 'big house', a lovely old Georgian mansion, was occupied, all was well. The Kellys had seen to his needs. But since the land had been sold, the house itself has been stripped bare, and the sheds are also falling into disrepair. Miriam had feared for 'The Dreamer', whose speech is peculiar and who makes little effort to communicate. So, having obtained a hut, she got permission from the Holy Ghost Fathers and from Mr Kelly, before the land was sold, to put it on the laneway between the two estates.

'The Dreamer' has not begun to use it yet, but when the property developers start work in earnest, he has a new home only thirty yards away from his old one. And Miriam is keeping an eye on him.

On our way to Foxrock, we stopped at the convent of the Daughters of the Cross. Pat knocked on the main door. She was looking for information about the people who came there to eat, as a survey of the 'outpeople' was being carried out.

'The convents do great work,' Miriam said. 'Many of these men would be hungry without them. And some of them strike up great relationships with particular nuns.'

She went on to talk about the incredible originality of some of her outmen.

'They are more akin to primitive men. They believe in strange beings in outer space and can communicate with them – like Ramouche Scarabanda from the star Samanka.'

'Who is he?' I asked, fascinated.

'Well people often call him Moses. You probably know him to see. He walks around Blackrock a good deal, wearing a blanket and carrying a stick. He is a truly biblical figure.'

'I'd love to have a chat with him,' I said.

'Well, maybe some day. You would have to be very discreet, though. He is very sensitive.'

At this point Pat returned. This convent had four regulars. She and Miriam were able to identify three of them by description. They wondered about the fourth. Passing Foxrock Church, Miriam said:

'The congregation in there would be shocked to know that the man we are going to visit now lives in such appalling conditions so close to them.'

But Máirtín was not in when we arrived. The little house was derelict. We had to climb up a muddy bank to get in. The main room was obviously inhabited. There was a chair, a mattress, odds and ends and a fireplace. It was very dirty. Miriam explained that they intended to clean up the room, glaze the window, and make it as comfortable as possible for him. He had only come out here recently. Máirtín is one of those who lives in a world of his own, which after all must be infinitely more pleasant for him than what we call the real world. He has a number of projects on hand. The most urgent at present is that of setting up a seaside resort in the little house on Westminster Road. Today, though, he must have been worried about air traffic control at Dublin Airport – or he might have stopped half-way on his long walk to check out a previous enterprise, a cafe in Drumcondra.

We came back into town through Ranelagh, keeping a lookout for the man we had met in St Stephen's Green earlier in the day. He was nowhere to be seen. Miriam remembered suddenly that she wanted to catch a young chap who always eats at a convent in Churchtown.

'He's mixed up in drugs,' she said. 'Only moved out of home recently. He's living in a skipper now. I want to help him get a flat. People need a hand at this stage before they sink too far.'

We missed him; he had come to the convent early. Miriam left a message for him.

'Now you are not to smile at anything our next man says,' Miriam warned me as we drove down the quays once again. 'St Satan lives in a skipper in the Park. We'll probably meet him walking now. He won't take food from anyone. He thinks a landlady tried to poison him once. I worry about him – he may not eat enough in the bad weather and if he ever had to be hospitalised he would probably starve to death.'

We saw him. I rolled down the car window. He started to talk immediately. He had been studying, had a lot of information now. As far as he could ascertain there were stars in the sky that were conspiring against the earth. They would fall down some day and stop the flow of water. There would be whole continents without water. There was a legacy due in 1943, he had been enquiring about it but nothing had happened yet. The Germans had been wrong in the eighteenth century . . .

A pleasant man with ruddy face and gentle eyes, he spoke so earnestly that he might have been pleading the most logical of cases in a court of law, but the logic was entirely his own. Miriam tried to get him to take a box of Alpen with him.

'It is like raw porridge. I have it myself for breakfast with cold milk poured over it.'

But no, that distant memory of the landlady with poisonous intent was too strong. He took his few pounds. He preferred to buy his own food. He trudged off along Parkgate Street, having at least unburdened his mind of some of its most urgent communications.

We decided to call it a day. Pat went off to meet a friend, Miriam wondered if someone had remembered to turn down the oven. It was 5.30 pm when we parted. She seemed tired. She spends most of her Sundays on Simon work. Sometimes she visits Mountjoy Prison, Dundrum Mental Hospital, or some of the other hospitals. Today had been a day for her outmen. In an article in the *Simon Community Newsletter*, she said of them:

> My men are law-abiding, more sinned against than sinning, dreamers and poets and gentle people, the victims of the avaricious unjust. I think St Jerome knew the aggressors well – 'Show me a rich man,' he said, 'and I will show you a thief or the son of a thief.' My men are innocent. Their eyes are full of wonder and their mouths are still wet with 'the milk of paradise'.

1

WHY SIMON?

One man's answer

Homelessness has been a feature of life in the British Isles as far back as medieval times, when laws were first passed for the punishment of vagrants, rogues, beggars and idle people, who were considered either a social nuisance or even a threat. In the nineteenth century the Poor Law Workhouses were instituted for the confinement of casuals, the mentally ill, and a ragbag of 'social misfits' from unmarried mothers to old people deserted by their relatives. Despite the fact that conditions in the workhouses were grim – they were designed to deter people who were not in real need – homelessness persisted into the twentieth century, and was the subject of government enquiries, censuses, and social literature before the First World War. There was the generally held belief after 1945 that homelessness would be eliminated in the course of the gigantic post-war housing programmes.

'To many politicians and social scientists,' David Brandon wrote,

> it seemed that homelessness had been washed away entirely by the development of the Welfare State – the flood of post-war social legislation let loose by the Labour Government.
>
> (*Guidelines to Research in Homelessness*, 1974, p. 1)

But this did not happen. In the late 1950s and early 1960s, shelters, hostels, and boarding accommodation remained as occupied as ever, filled mainly with homeless single men in their thirties, forties and fifties. So while the majority of British citizens were enjoying the relative affluence of the post-war era, there was an ever-growing number who simply could not cope with the demands and pressures of life in a complex society. They were slipping through the net of the welfare system and were quickly becoming forgotten citizens.

Anton Wallich-Clifford was, at this time, serving as a probation officer to the Chief Metropolitan Magistrate's Court at Bow Street in London. A tall, bearded man, he walked with a slight stoop. Despite his stern physical appearance, he became involved with many of his clients. They called without appointment and he made time to see them. Many of them were of no fixed abode. He began to realise that getting a placement and a bed for some of them was not the answer. The chilling reality was that homelessness for some was not primarily a matter of accommodation, but was in fact a symptom of a deeper problem, which he eventually came to recognise as 'social inadequacy'. Little in his training had prepared him for this; it was the homeless themselves who taught him the meaning of inadequacy:

> I very quickly began to understand that the overt demand for a bed chit or a pair of shoes was no more than the formality of an introduction – a way of gaining some sort of acceptance. It was an inarticulate cry from the heart for recognition as a human being, and not just as a figure in the queue waiting for a handout. What was really wanted was a quiet half an hour in the warm, with a fag and an attentive listening ear; an atmosphere as different as possible from the dismal disinfected corridors of doss-houses. . . . Above all to establish some sort of relationship, however impermanent, so that one could come again and be known by name and not as a bed number.
>
> (*No Fixed Abode*, London, Macmillan, 1974, p. 18)

So Anton began to take the initiative – and in a daring and costly manner. On a number of evenings a week, instead of going home, he donned his 'skipper gear' and set out for the underworld of London. He went to the parks and the bomb-sites, the derelict houses and the all-night cafes, in order to make friends with the homeless. Some of them he knew from the courts; others had never been in trouble with the law but the chances were that they would be in the future unless someone heeded their plight. Men and women, young and old, these were the people at the bottom of the pile. Unkempt in appearance, gruff in manner, their behaviour often appeared anti-social in a society where good manners and conventions counted for so much. Anton met them on their own ground. He tried to blend with the atmosphere. He came back again and again. He slept rough with these social outcasts. Gradually he gained their trust.

Another outcome of his experiment was that he began to have some inkling of what it *felt* like to be homeless. Not to be able to wash or shave easily, to be so cold at night that a bottle of wine was necessary to induce sleep, to be aware of people in the street turning away from you in disgust or embarrassment, these were the realities of what it meant to be homeless in London. 'Dossers' often tended to be treated without dignity by the law, by casualty departments in hospitals, by ministers of religion, by social security officials. At every turn they experienced society as being hostile to them. Small wonder, then, that they in turn rejected society and its institutions. They were not prepared to take the initiative any longer, even in seeking help.

A novel approach was necessary if their real needs were to be met. These needs were basic: food, clothing, shelter, and above all warm, human companionship. How could these be provided in a manner which would prove acceptable to the people of London's underworld? Anton struggled with this question for quite some time. His personal contribution to the 'answer' was to found the Simon Community in 1963. He had already resigned from the probation service the previous year, to take up a post as a founding warden of a residential half-way house for ex-prisoners in Southampton. But he felt he must go further. With the birth of the Simon Community, Anton's commitment to the homeless and friendless became total. He no longer had a career in the ordinary sense; Simon was to be his way of life.

A sense of direction

Caring and campaigning were the twin pillars on which Simon was built. Community, which in essence meant the helpers and the homeless living a communal life, was to be the heart of the movement. Anton brought the diverse strands of his experience and study together when working out the philosophy of this new venture. His ultimate aim was to work towards the establishment of a caring society, where neighbourliness and community action would respond to the needs of those at risk. His immediate aim was twofold. New ventures in caring had to be set up in order to provide for the homeless who had no sense of belonging to the society in which they existed, and in order to make that society more aware of their plight, a national alerting campaign had to be launched.

Anton, with his mother and the other early members of Simon, set out to live in community. This they did initially in a small flat in St Leonard's-on-Sea, Sussex, which formed the administrative base for some months. As yet they had no clients. They had to wait to find a suitable premises. But the campaigning and fund-raising work began; they printed leaflets and a newsletter in which Anton explored and developed the ideas and principles of this new community for the homeless and rootless, which was to be called Simon. The name came naturally. Familiar with the Passion accounts in the Gospels, Anton felt that the stranger from Cyrene, who was compelled to help Jesus carry his cross, would be a suitable patron. Simon, too, was an unknown citizen; we do not hear of him again. But he helped in the hour of need, and that was what the Simon Community wished to do.

After eight hectic and often frustrating months, Simon opened its first house at 129 Malden Road in London. Here the philosophy of caring, which had been so carefully worked out, was first put into practice. The volunteers lived in community with a few of the homeless, who were busy using their wits in testing out this 'house of hospitality'. The first residents came because they knew and trusted Anton. Gradually others heard about Simon, and dropped in for what became known as the 'midnight soup-sessions' or a 'one night floor space'.

The house was run in a permissive fashion. People were accepted as they were, there was little attempt to impose standards of behaviour. The volunteers did their best to identify with the residents by wearing old clothes, accepting the same living conditions and surviving on a small pocket money allowance. At first sight it would have been difficult to be sure who were the helpers. The rationale behind the functioning of the house was the belief that community living could be therapeutic. Enlightened psychological theories of the day, most notably those of Maxwell Jones, suggested that people with personality disorders could be healed, to some degree at least, by living in a community atmosphere, and learning to participate in decision-making which affected their own life-styles. The house at Malden Road offered its residents a sense of belonging and a say in how things were run. Of course people came and went. There were problems of noise and violence when residents were drunk. Helpers were often saddened when an alcoholic went boozing again after many weeks on the dry. But it was a time of great excitement. A new idea had been tried, and it was working. Men who had never stayed in hostels, or trusted anyone, were giving Simon a chance, and growing as a result.

Anton had not set out to rehabilitate people, but simply to let them know that someone did care, that they were not living in a totally hostile world. He was the central figure in the house and despite his time-consuming involvement in fund-raising and public relations work for Simon, he was never too busy to have a chat with a friend, or to spend the long night hours with a resident going through a crisis.

The tier system was part of the Simon vision from the early days. Those who used the house at Malden Road had diverse needs. Anton was concerned to interpret these needs and thus to initiate different types of residential communities. Houses of hospitality and night-shelters were involved in first-tier work; the priorities at this level were a place to sleep, plentiful food, and an atmosphere of warmth and friendliness. Few demands were made on residents and callers. They would stay, it was hoped, because they felt accepted and 'at home'. Often crowded and apparently chaotic, first-tier houses attempted to create a non-threatening environment with little stress on the niceties of social living.

After a period in the first-tier house, some residents were ready to move on to what might be seen as a half-way house. In a second-tier community, members would have a greater opportunity to participate in the day-to-day running of their house. Greater stress would be laid on comfort and the general quality of life. Some residents might be employed outside; others would have specific jobs within the house. As people would only join at their own request, Anton hoped that this type of house would be partly funded by the residents themselves, and that each member of the community would take some responsibility for creating a caring atmosphere. Having spent a period at second-tier level, various possibilities would be open to the resident. He might return by choice to a first-tier house, or if in need of long-term supportive care, he could move on to a third-tier community, which ideally would be situated in a rural area, and incorporate some kind of work project.

Anton was concerned that only those in genuine need of permanent Simon care would use the third tier; he had no wish to work with those who would do just as well in other establishments. Simon had been founded to work with those with whom no-one else was working, and duplication would simply mean a waste of valuable resources. There were a few residents who returned to 'normal society' after a spell in a second-tier house, but they were the minority. This was due largely to the fact that returning to society often meant returning to the loneliness of a bedsitter. As isolation seemed to be the root cause of social inadequacy, it was little wonder that few survived the move.

This realisation sparked off the idea of the fourth tier, which was meant to operate as an 'extended community'. Quite simply, this meant having a number of individuals living in lodgings or bedsitters in a specific location, who could be in touch with an advice centre in the area run by Simon workers. In these circumstances the people concerned had their own space, but they knew that they were not completely alone.

This tier system did not run like clockwork. Systems, however well devised, must always be tempered by the reality of the people they set out to serve. Simon was no exception; the residents could not be easily arranged into neat groups. They themselves and the volunteers had to use the trial and error method when trying to establish what kind of living situation was best suited to their needs. Mistakes were made. Nevertheless, in the early years, the tier system ensured that the volunteers were not working in a theoretical vacuum.

That Anton was able to work out the ground rules for such a comprehensive system of caring in the early sixties was a major achievement. His vision was inspirational, if not always thoroughly practical. Having been inspired by radical ventures in care in Europe and America, he was determined to initiate a movement with direction.

Outstanding among those who influenced him was Dorothy Day, who, with Peter Maurin, founded the Catholic Worker Movement in the USA in the 1930s. They attempted to combat poverty by running houses of hospitality for those on skid row, houses in which the workers lived a life of voluntary poverty. A professional journalist herself, Dorothy also stressed the need for a campaign. She was editor of the *Catholic Worker*, a free newspaper, which encouraged the oppressed themselves to unite and take action in order to improve their lot. When in 1964, Anton saw the need for a readable and image-creating publication, it was to the *Catholic Worker* he turned for inspiration. What emerged was the *Simon Star*, a paper designed to keep the various Simon supporters in touch and to spread the message to a wider public.

Fertile soil

The Simon Community spread like wildfire throughout England and Scotland during the sixties. Anton's unflagging energy and his extraordinary ability as a public speaker, which enabled him to communicate immediately with his listeners, were major contributory factors. Yet Simon did not develop quite as he might have wished. What he had originally envisaged was something akin to a religious community, where some members, at least, would commit themselves permanently to living and working with the homeless. But Simon did not have the stability of a religious order, nor did it only attract those who wished to do the work for religious motives. Although Christian in its inspiration, it drew both workers and residents from all religions and none. Ironically, this non-denominationalism was perhaps its greatest strength, at a time when young people in Britain were challenging the political and religious values of their parents' generation.

Radical youth movements mushroomed during the sixties. The atmosphere was one of confidence and optimism. A new sense of the brotherhood of all mankind prevailed. Protest groups sprang up around such issues as nuclear warfare, apartheid in South Africa and American involvement in

Vietnam. On the home front, there was growing disillusionment with conventional politics. Young people felt alienated by a political system which did not offer the possibility of full participation. They were making their presence felt through public demonstrations about specific issues. Students were more affluent than their predecessors had been; for some, participation in the youth revolt was merely a passing fad, but for the more reflective among them it became a political act. An awareness was growing that behind the affluent façade lay the realities of poverty, homelessness, environmental destruction and the continuing emergence of a grey and alienating industrial society. There was an increasing desire among the young to challenge the structures of this society which was entrenching social divisions and frustrating the evolution of a genuine democracy where people could control their own lives.

The enthusiasm and deep commitment which characterises radical movements was to become a feature of Simon. For many young idealists in the sixties, volunteer work in a community house was a form of political statement. The concept of a person-to-person care, stressing as it did the dignity of each individual, however battered by life, caught on quickly. The group structure of the houses, based on democratic meetings where both residents and workers had an equal say, appealed to those who believed that in the new society, democracy would mean not only participation by those in government, but by every member of society.

All kinds of organisational problems arose. Simon spread too rapidly in the first two years and had to go through a period of retrenchment, when all the houses except the original one on Malden Road had to be closed down. Nevertheless, by 1969 there were Simon projects in Liverpool, Exeter, Glasgow, Edinburgh, Oxford and Cambridge, as well as a number of houses in London. Anton had accepted the changes which had overtaken the Community. On the campaigning front, success was the order of the day, according to Anton's own assessment:

> The voluntary homeless movement was well and truly launched. The dosser and the skipper were newsworthy; social workers, even those not associated with this type

> of work, could hardly escape the amount of written material relating to the problem, and certainly recognised that homelessness concerned them all. Local authorities and central government, alerted to the need, began slowly but surely to make provision.
>
> (*Caring on Skid Row*, Dublin, Veritas, 1976, pp. 26-27)

Despite differences, related mainly to practical matters, which led to breakaway groups like the Cyrenians, and new ventures founded by ex-Simon workers such as the St Mungo Community, Simon had achieved much of what it had set out to do. Not only had Anton given birth to Simon, but the Simon Community in Britain had itself conceived a number of new projects suited to local needs.

Dublin 1969 . . . taking the initiative

One evening in February 1969, a poster in Earlsfort Terrace caught the attention of a nineteen-year-old social science student. It was advertising a talk which was to be given by Anton Wallich-Clifford on the subject of the Irish homeless and rootless in Britain. The student was Larry Masterson, a dynamic young Dubliner, with curly hair, a warm manner, and an intense desire to improve the lot of those who were called the 'less fortunate members of society'. He attended the talk and it fired his imagination.

Anton spoke with great power, painting a moving picture of London's underworld, which included among its population a high proportion of Irish emigrants. He went on to explain the philosophy of the Simon Community, paying particular attention to the notion of taking the initiative. Those who most needed help did not seek it. It was necessary to go out, find them and offer them friendship on their own terms. He described the different Simon projects operating in England and made an impassioned plea for Irish volunteers to come and work with their compatriots in Britain.

Larry's thoughts were moving in a different direction. If this was the situation in Britain, was it not also probable that there might be a similar problem in Dublin, of which no-one was aware. When the meeting was over he talked to Anton about the possibility of setting up a like organisation in Dublin. The following morning he and a few friends made the initial plans over a cup of coffee in the student canteen.

About a fortnight later a public meeting, which had been well advertised, was held in the Arts Society rooms in Trinity College. This was attended mainly by students. The atmosphere was one of excitement and goodwill. Many of those present were studying psychology or social science and the challenge of some practical work along radical lines was very appealing. An *ad hoc* committee was formed, but it did not have much power. This was the era when democracy was a sacred word among Dublin students, and democracy meant that everyone had a say in every decision. Larry Masterson, however, was the undisputed leader; he was also the direct link with Anton. A basic plan of action resulted from that meeting.

It was decided to start a soup-run, which would go out three times a week between 9 pm and 3 am to different areas around the city in search of people sleeping rough. Volunteers were to bring soup with them, and with this as an introduction, attempt to initiate a relationship with those whom they visited. Great emphasis was laid on a willingness to listen patiently.

At the beginning the soup-run would be run in conjunction with a survey as it was necessary to establish how many people were actually sleeping rough around Dublin. Volunteers were to approach local Gardaí or other officials who might have information concerning the whereabouts of such people. Premises were needed to use as a soup-kitchen, where the volunteers would meet to prepare the soup before going out on the run. Someone from Voluntary Services International who was present offered the use of their basement in Merrion Square. The date of the first soup-run was decided upon and it was agreed that a report would be written about the happenings of each nightly run.

To conduct a survey of people sleeping rough, in an area as vast as Dublin city, would be a daunting task even for a professional team. Such a professional survey was subsequently carried out, in July 1971, by Séamus Ó Cinnéide and Peter Mooney. It involved months of planning, but its principal resource at the outset was the information and expertise which Simon workers had built up over the previous two years.

The volunteers in early 1969 had no such expertise to

draw on; they were armed only with goodwill and determination. Their enthusiasm knew no bounds. Night after night they set out, on foot, on motorbikes, occasionally by car, to comb the streets and laneways of the inner city, the canal bank from Mount Street to Dolphin's Barn, the vast expanses of the Phoenix Park, and the derelict houses and abandoned cars in the Smithfield area. They found the homeless: men and women, young and old, from rural and urban backgrounds. It is difficult to establish exactly the number of people contacted in the early days. One report, written by Ray Clarke, a psychology student at that time, states:

> The initial survey uncovered about fifty people in three days but subsequent events lead us to believe that at least one hundred people sleep out in Dublin at night.
> ('Report from the gutter', *Simon Newsletter*, 1969, p. 1)

Another student, Denis Cahalane, who became the first treasurer of Dublin Simon, told me that in some instances over-enthusiastic volunteers insisted on feeding soup and sandwiches to young lads coming home drunk from dances at around 2 am, convinced that they were hopeless winos! Nevertheless, a lot of valuable information was gathered in the early weeks, and some of those who are now alive and well and living in Simon were contacted at that time.

As more people became committed to the idea, the soup-run began to go out every night. Among the soup-runners at this stage were a number of young men who were homeless themselves. Having enjoyed the soup and sandwiches and the company of the volunteers on a few occasions, they decided that they would like to help out. Their contribution was invaluable, as they knew the locations of the less-obvious skippers (term used by the homeless for a makeshift sleeping place), and because of their presence, the Simon volunteers were considered trustworthy by some who might otherwise have rejected any form of help.

A problem arose, however, when the soup-run finished each night; the volunteers had homes or flats to go to, but these lads had nowhere. Watching them head off for a skipper at 3 am in harsh weather made some of the students feel very guilty. This was the beginning of a realisation that was to dominate meetings and discussions elsewhere for the rest of the year – Simon needed a residential house, somewhere where these lads could sleep and where others could come if they grew tired of sleeping rough.

In an effort to focus public attention on the plight of the homeless, a twenty-four-hour fast was held in May 1969, which incorporated a night 'sleeping rough' outside the main gates of St Stephen's Green. The *Irish Press* of May 15 covered this event. The headline was 'New Hope for Social Outcasts'. The first paragraph of the article reflected two features which were to characterise much of the early publicity received by Simon. Firstly, the facts reported were inaccurate, because any Simon volunteer at the time was happy to speak to a reporter, giving his or her own personal view of the situation. Secondly, the language used by many reporters to describe Simon work tended to be highly emotive. The paragraph to which I refer reads:

> Unofficial help is on the way for the 400 pathetic drop-outs of Dublin's unrecognised Skid Row – and the rescuers are launching their mission of mercy by attempting to put the people of Dublin to shame.

This kind of publicity, however, was not without its benefits. Donations began to arrive – money, food, old clothes, even a van in working order. Erin Foods Ltd donated whatever soup was needed; other companies proved equally generous.

At the beginning of the summer, the soup-run moved its headquarters from the Voluntary Service International premises to the Arts Society rooms in Trinity College. They were allowed to use this building for the duration of the college holidays on condition that no one should be allowed to sleep there. Group meetings were held regularly in order to discuss policy; at this time there were about fifty people actively involved. Others often turned up to the meetings, where issues were endlessly discussed and decisions were rarely made. It was hardly coincidental that many of the UCD students involved were members of the radical group, Students for Democratic Action, which had staged the famous sit-in in the college in March of that year. Jim Murray, a twenty-four-year old engineer with the Department of Posts and Telegraphs, was one of the first non-students to become actively involved. In June he went out on his first soup-run.

'I only remember it vaguely. We went up Parkgate Street, and out to the Conyngham Road bus station. I remember meeting a guy called Jimmy, who was very, very, gentle, completely different from my image of dossers, one of the gentlest people I've ever met.'

Jim had a clearer memory of his impressions of the meetings held in the Arts Society rooms.

'At that time Simon was quite disorganised, even more than it has ever been since. There were various people there who were self-styled anarchists, who did not agree with taking decisions on things. They seemed to have a rigid objection to policy of any kind – 'though maybe it was just the sixties.'

Simon, by the late summer of 1969, had already made a considerable impact. Those sleeping rough had become accustomed to the greeting, 'Hello, it's Simon, would you like some soup?' The Irish public were becoming aware of a new kind of social problem in their midst. Simon itself was still predominantly a student organisation and its main concern was to find premises from which to operate, which would serve both as a soup-kitchen and as a house of hospitality where volunteers and residents could live together in community.

2

PUTTING DOWN THE ROOTS

In search of a roof

The early Simon workers discovered that Dublin had its own underworld. Here too, there were forgotten citizens, who were not being catered for by any of the existing agencies. They slept rough in various areas around the city. Some of them were loners; they proved difficult to find. Others formed loosely-knit groups and tended to skipper in a particular area.

One such location was the neighbourhood around Smithfield on the north side of the Liffey which during the day was alive with all the hustle and bustle associated with fruit and vegetable markets in any big city. At night, however, it became 'home' for a group of men and women, most of whom were wine drinkers. They slept in the abandoned cars, stuffing the broken windows with old newspapers to keep out the wind and rain.

Their days were spent between begging and tramping the streets in search of the best dinner houses. Sometimes a couple of them were to be seen sitting on a city pavement, drinking wine straight from the bottle. Towards evening they might congregate on some piece of waste ground and light a fire. Here they would while away the hours, sharing their fags and whatever food they might have. Someone might have a bottle or two to pass around. There were fights too. Some individuals took offence easily; physical violence could erupt within seconds.

When the fire died down they would head for 'home', and, with the help of cardboard, newspapers and old overcoats, they would make themselves as comfortable as possible for the night, hoping that sleep would come quickly and last until morning.

Life was rough, yet they had each other; they formed a kind of community. After a spell in Mountjoy Jail or St Brendan's Psychiatric Hospital, they were welcomed back to the group. They had little contact with 'the other world' in which ordinary people lived. They distrusted policemen and doctors and the law; for the most part they had every reason to do so. Then the soup-runners arrived, a strange group of young people, who chatted to them and appeared to treat them with respect.

'We didn't know what to expect,' one man told me. 'A van pulled up, and they used to go around the cars with soup, sandwiches, old clothes and maybe a few blankets or anything like that to warm you up. We began to expect them then, the Simons. They didn't come every night, though.'

As time went on, the wine drinkers began to look forward to meeting these young people, who told them all about Anton and the founding of Simon in England. The volunteers had a dream at this time: they wanted a house in which to create a therapeutic community. They shared their dream with the men and women they visited at night. It formed a bond between them, this hope that some day they would live together in a house, where there would be no rules, a little bit of comfort and a sense of togetherness.

But by the end of September 1969 the volunteers found themselves without even a headquarters. They had to move out of the Arts Society rooms as the new college term was beginning. For a short time they used a premises in Drumcondra, but they were feeling really frustrated. Aware now of the extent of the problem, they were longing to be in a position to meet more fully the needs of their new-found friends.

One journalist who had taken an interest in the work of the organisation was the late Eileen O'Brien of the *Irish Times*. In May she had written extensively about the soup-run in 'A Social Sort of Column'. She proved to be a valuable contact, as it was through an appeal made by her in the *Irish Times* in October 1969 that Simon obtained their next soup-kitchen.

Frank O'Leary, a Franciscan priest in his early forties, was at this time stationed at the friary in Merchant's Quay. Having previously been involved in education, he had moved into pastoral work, and was coming to the conviction that the Church should be working with the poor. He saw Eileen

O'Brien's appeal and wrote to her, offering the use of an upstairs room, containing both sink and cooker, in a disused house in Winetavern Street, owned by the Franciscans. Eileen contacted Simon about the offer and as a result Frank had a meeting with Larry Masterson and Mary Goshan, an English woman who had devoted a great deal of time and energy to the administrative side of the organisation.

They were delighted with the kitchen and began to use it immediately. Frank used to go over at night when they were making the soup. He enjoyed meeting the young people, but had no intention of becoming involved in the actual work. One night, however, only two soup-runners turned up, neither of whom had a car. They waited around until midnight; then Frank suggested that he would drive them around. They were not keen on the idea, mainly because they were scared that 'Father' was going to come in his Franciscan habit! He did go, and remembered that he found the night a terrifying experience.

'It was dark up in Smithfield; when we stopped, about sixteen people emerged out of the shadows and hung around the car. At least three or four times it came to the brink of a row – then someone would say, "Cool it, Paddy". Somehow we survived. I just stayed in the background, not wanting to remain an onlooker, but being extremely cautious nevertheless. I just didn't know how to deal with these people.'

However, when the soup-runners were stuck for a car after that, they called on Frank. Eventually he decided to commit himself to one night a week – by this time the volunteers went out every night. Frank became a Thursday night soup-runner and a fully fledged member of the Simon Community. He had become involved, almost by accident, in an organisation which was to claim much of his energy.

Once again Simon had a soup-kitchen; once again they received it on condition that no one should sleep there at night. This was beginning to pose a real problem. The volunteers were conscious of how little they had to offer. On the soup-run they often met people who were desperately in need of temporary accommodation. They could not refer them anywhere late at night. It was impossible to ignore some of them. Jim Murray remembers one occasion when he broke the rule and allowed someone to stay in the house.

'I found a girl of about fifteen outside the Regina Coeli [Hostel], I think she was pregnant. She had just come up from the country, had got lost and had arrived at the hostel fifteen minutes after closing time. She had two or three suitcases. I brought her back and left her in the house on her own as I had to get up for work in the morning. I rang Frank afterwards to apologise and explain. I don't think that was the first time it happened. But the rule began to be broken more and more – by any soup-runner who felt sad about a person being out on the street, but it was not formal policy.'

At one stage the volunteers were worried about a man who was sleeping in a barn in Milltown Park. He was extremely ill, but would not hear of going to a hospital. They had the idea that he might come first to Winetavern Street, and once there they would be better able to coax him into hospital. Frank O'Leary approached his superior, Fr Giblin, about this matter. Because he had previously worked in Camden Town, and was aware of the kind of problems the Simon workers were up against, Fr Giblin proved sympathetic and gave his permission, provided Simon would be prepared to move out when requested, as he had plans about restructuring the house. The committee of the time agreed to this.

John, from Milltown, came to stay in the house and eventually went to hospital. At the same time, the three young men who had been helping the soup-runners from the beginning moved in and settled there. Others heard the news and came looking for shelter. Gradually it became a residential house; there were people there during the day and at night. By Christmas of 1969, it had become a makeshift community with Charlie, one of the young men, acting as unofficial house-leader.

Home and dry

As the number of residents in the Winetavern Street house grew, so did the chaos. The volunteers spent a lot of time on the premises, trying to keep the peace and to introduce some kind of order, but it became obvious fairly quickly that there was a genuine need for someone to be there and in control all of the time. Full-time workers were needed. A great deal of soul-searching went on among the members; finally Jim Murray volunteered. He decided to apply for six months leave of absence from the civil service, and in early January of 1970 he went off to London to visit Malden Road, and to spend some time with Jim Horne of the St Mungo Community in order to get the feel of a residential house.

When he returned he discovered that he would not be alone. John Long, a twenty year old social science student, had decided to give up his studies and become a full-time worker. He had worked on building sites in London before going to college, and, having been involved in the soup-run for a few months, he felt that Simon had more to offer him at that time than an academic course. He commanded a great deal of respect from the residents because of his patience and warmth; these qualities together with his calm courage in the face of physical violence made him an ideal Simon worker. He and Jim struck up a good relationship quickly and worked well as a team over a six-month period. Jim described how they divided the responsibilities between them.

'The real story of the first six months and later is of John Long. He towered over everybody and got all the bad jobs. I had the cream – PR work, on TV, going to dinners and speaking. I had a car and could always find some excuse to be away from the house. John had none of these perks. His influence on the residents was uncanny – many of them would be upset on his day off. He was the rock on which the whole thing was built.'

In those early days, the house was teeming with all kinds of different people. On the one hand, there was a feeling that no one should be refused help by Simon. As a result young prostitutes, runaway kids, and some genuinely dangerous characters were taken in at various stages. On the other hand, once Jim and John had been in control for a while, they were able to assess the situation more clearly and they did begin to make decisions as to whom should be allowed in.

At the heart of the community was the group of wine drinkers, who had found a new home. Many of that original group are dead now; some stayed with Simon right to the end. John Joe was one of those who moved up from Smithfield at the beginning. I asked him what difference the move had made to him.

'It was terrific, getting out of them cars. I'll tell you why – you couldn't stretch your legs in the cars. And when you woke up in the morning you weren't only cold but you were stiff in the legs. It was really good living in that house – something I couldn't explain. You had a roof over your head, you had a home, although you were only sleeping on a mattress on the floor. It was great luxury.'

He went on to tell me some of his memories of those days.

'There was a great mixture there, like – women and men. A lot of them there jumped in the Liffey. Poor old Happy O'Rourke, Happy was found in the Liffey drowned after five days. It's all the wine you see. It was a good community of people, you know. We were rough and ready. The women and men, we all slept in the same rooms – there was no messing or carrying on like. And there was the old Boxer – an ex-army man he was. He was the cook and you daren't go near the kitchen. If you put your hand over on the food he'd take it off with a knife. He was a great character. There was a piano there and we used to have singsongs. But then the priest took the piano away – he had to take it back. As he was taking it down the stairs, I was still playing it. The workers were alright. They'd let you in drunk, but they wouldn't let you carry a bottle in. They didn't like violence, but there was violence, ah there was. You know what it's like when people get drink inside them.'

The house in Winetavern Street was not physically suited as a house of hospitality. A narrow, four storey building, it was unfurnished when Simon moved in. The upstairs kitchen continued to be used by the soup-runners. Other rooms were used as sleeping quarters. The windows were constantly getting broken and often remained that way due to lack of finance. They washed the house down every second day and tried to change the blankets as often as possible. The workers were operating on the Simon principle that no resident could be separated from his or her pet; as a result there were quite a number of dogs around, none of whom was house-trained.

Jim and John remained the two key figures. Gradually the power, which had rested with Larry Masterson and various *ad hoc* committees, came to be theirs. Jim, who was both shrewd and competent, realised that there was a need for a sound structure; he set about investigating the possibility of forming a limited company.

By this stage, a few older influential people had become interested in the work of the community. Professor Kaim-Caudle, a visiting academic, whose daughter was friendly with Larry Masterson, enlisted the aid of the late Bob Cashman, a civil servant in the Department of Local Government and a high-ranking member of the St Vincent de Paul Society. Meanwhile, the late Frank Sweeney, a solicitor in his early forties, came along to a meeting to see if he could be of assistance. He went out on the soup-run for a while – soup-runners with cars were always popular. He also spent a fair amount of time in the house. He and Bob were to become two vital characters in the development of Simon during the early seventies.

Denis Cahalane was treasurer at this time and by all accounts he was a tough one. There was never a great deal of money in the kitty; Denis felt that they should spend as little as possible. They only bought whatever food was absolutely necessary. In true Simon style, they went to the markets a couple of times a week and begged as much as they could in the line of fruit, vegetables and meat. Bread came free from a bakery in Church Street, soup from Erin soups, tinned food from Batchelors of Bannow Road. The residents were involved in the hunt for food and occasionally there would be a question mark over the nature of the transactions conducted. John Long had memories about this:

'People would go out and arrive back with ten or twelve huge boxes of cornflakes which had fallen off the back of a lorry! Nobody asked any questions. There were some luxuries in life, though. There was a co-worker whose family controlled the Ovaltine Company, so there was a plentiful supply of Ovaltine. On Saturday mornings we used to have tomatoes on toast with pepper and oregano on top – that was delicious.'

Talking to some of those who were residents at this period, I got a tremendous sense of their pride in the whole enterprise. They were consulted and had a say in what was happening. Charlie, who had been the unofficial house leader before Jim and John came in full-time, continued to function as a worker for quite some time. He was handy and took to collecting scrap copper from which he and some of the residents made jewellery. Jimmy, another of the younger men, also acted as a worker for a period; but this blurring of the demarcation between worker and resident did not really work out in the long term. When situations of conflict arose, Jack and Jimmy were unable to be impartial; their old loyalties won out and they would take sides with one group of residents against another. Eventually they both left the house.

One resident, who was a central character at this time, has remained one of the constants in the Simon story throughout the years. Tommy would have been about forty-five then, a well-built man of immense physical strength. He had been in Daingean Reformatory for three years in his early teens and has terrible memories of the brutality of the place.

'We were tough kids,' he told me, 'but you can only take so much.'

From then on there was a pattern to his life. Much of his time was spent in prison; while inside he was dry, once out he was back on the wine and sleeping rough. He distrusted the Simon people at first.

'That particular night I'd never heard of Simon and when the two men approached me in the car, I was under the opinion that they were detectives. "I've had it now," I said to myself. They asked me if I wanted a bed. I said I did, but not in the Bridewell. "Oh no," they said, "we're Simon." They told me they had a house in Winetavern Street. I'd get a mattress on the floor, a cup of tea and whatever else was going. So I took a chance. They put me into a car and brought me down.'

Tommy was happy in Winetavern Street. He could be very violent when he was drunk, but as the workers grew to know his ways they were able to deal with him. He spent long periods on the dry; at those times he needed something to do during the day. He enjoyed making the copper jewellery, particularly when they had got a stall going in the Dandelion Market, where they could sell their wares. He remembers suggesting that they should collect old paperbacks from the volunteers in order to make a few bob for Simon. He also went out in the Simon van to help collect furniture or old clothes or whatever was coming their way.

Marie O'Donoghue was the first female full-time worker in Dublin Simon. She threw in her lot with the others and slept on a mattress on the floor. A nineteen year old, she had previously been working as a shorthand typist. She, too, had been involved in the soup-run and was a part-time worker in the house for the first few months. Once she saw she could be of use, she decided to give up her job in order to work full-time for Simon. Jim and John both remember her as an 'extraordinarily beautiful girl, who was extremely competent.' In an interview given to the *Irish Independent* on June 24th 1970, she said:

> Simon offers us a sense of involvement that we cannot find in other organisations. Here we have time to talk and communicate with the people.

At that time people just decided to become workers; there was no selection procedure. This worried Jim and John, who had a fair idea as to who would be suitable, but because of the democratic nature of the organisation, it was difficult for them to implement any particular policy in relation to workers. Jim was determined, though, to formalise Simon as an organisation by having it set up as a limited company. He saw the necessity for continuity. Workers would come and go, he realised, and unless there was a company structure, with an Executive Committee, there would always be the danger that the organisation would simply fizzle out. He was shrewd enough also to realise that while the idea of young students devoting themselves tirelessly to the plight of the down and out might appeal to the emotions of the public, another kind of image was necessary before it was possible to encourage donations from business men, or to conduct negotiations with statutory bodies.

Frank Sweeney looked after the legal side; a Memorandum and Articles of Association were drawn up by his office. Frank himself became chairman. Bob Cashman, who had successfully negotiated with Dublin Corporation for two houses in Sarsfield Quay, became vice chairman. Jim Murray, John Long and Denis Cahalane, who had by this stage become a full-time worker, were also subscribers. The two remaining signatures on the document were those of Croasdella Cruess-Callaghan and Séamus Ó Cinnéide. Croasdella had offered her services as a fund-raiser and eventually became treasurer. Séamus, who was working with the Institute of Public Administration at the time, had a background in social policy and administration. Knowing how hostels were normally administered, he was excited by the unconditional acceptance of the Simon approach, and had become involved initially as a soup-runner. These seven, then, were the original directors. The document was dated September 9th 1970. By this time both Jim and John had resigned from full-time work; they left, feeling that the organisation had a sound administrative base.

An important development

Sarsfield Quay, on the north side of the River Liffey, and within a stone's throw of Heuston Station, was the location of the two newly acquired houses. They were in bad repair. The St Vincent de Paul Society was prepared to finance the renovation of both houses as well as an extension to No 9, providing showers and toilets. However, on account of a long cement strike, it was not until January 1971 that the house in Winetavern Street was vacated. Jim Murray had left in June by which time Denis Cahalane had settled in as a full-time worker. John Long lasted until August; by that stage he was physically and emotionally exhausted. Other workers came along.

In the autumn of 1970 the team would have consisted of Denis and Marie, two young Scotsmen, Jock Maguire and Andy Cooper, Rita Deegan, who had been a part-timer for a long period, and Ray Smyth, who was also familiar with the residents before becoming a full-time worker. Meanwhile there had been an important development. A social psychologist, employed by The Economic and Social Research Institute, had taken an interest in the project.

Ian Hart was thirty years of age and married when, in the summer of 1970, he was approached by a member of Simon and asked if he would like to become involved in the work of the Community. He accepted the invitation. As a social psychologist he was attracted to the idea of studying Simon's approach to its residents. He had an interest in the area of social deviance, having already done research concerning deprived children within the residential care system. Involvement with Dublin Simon now offered him the opportunity of working with 'difficult and apparently unmanageable adults' outside a traditional institutional setting.

In addition to his academic training in psychology, Ian Hart had undergone psychoanalysis in order to gain first-hand knowledge of psychoanalytic concepts. He was, therefore, able to offer considerable expertise as a psychotherapist to Dublin Simon. He was of the opinion that psychotherapy could have positive significance for many of the Simon residents. What he envisaged in fact was a therapeutic community approach, where people might learn about their attitudes to life through an examination of their relationships with one another. The first Simon house in Malden Road, London, had already made use of the idea that community living could be therapeutic. Ian was prepared to take this idea a step further by attempting group psychotherapy sessions within Dublin Simon. He got involved, realising that he would be a professional among volunteers, but this prospect did not daunt him. In an article written seven years later he stated his position on this issue:

> Both the dedicated volunteer and the 'mercenary' professional have a place in the Simon Community. The volunteer is needed for his personal commitment to the underprivileged; the professional for his relevant skills and expertise. Without the poorly paid voluntary worker, there might be a growing institutionalisation; without the professional, there might be the tendency to identify with the client to such an extent that the worker might lose his own values.
> ('Dedicated volunteer or mercenary professional', *Simon Ireland Newsletter*, February 1976)

The workers in Winetavern Street were not so sure of Ian, though, when he first arrived. He was, after all, a professional psychologist and much to their dismay introduced himself as such to workers and residents alike. He visited the house frequently in the autumn of 1970 in an attempt to familiarise himself with the situation, and to get to know the people involved.

Then, coincidentally, another professional became involved. Dermot McMahon, a young psychiatric nurse, who had been indulging in a period of voluntary unemployment, accidentally heard of the Simon Community. Having trained in Dublin in the early sixties, Dermot had worked in a number of mental institutions in England, experience which culminated in a two-year period in the Henderson Hospital in Surrey. This was a unit which specialised in the treatment of young people with personality disorders. It was run on democratic lines and did not use drugs or physical treatment of any kind. Patients were encouraged to think for themselves and a conscious effort was made to liberate people rather than to let them become dependent.

Dermot had enjoyed working there and became convinced of the validity of this particular therapeutic approach. So, on his return to Ireland, he was interested in finding a project which would allow him to work along these lines. When Ian and Dermot met, they found they had a great deal in common. They began to explore the idea of setting up a therapeutic community within Simon.

Some of the full-time workers, notably Ray Smyth and Rita Deegan, were very excited at the prospect of the move to Sarsfield Quay, with the possibility of setting up a 'dry house'. A few of the wine drinkers were making a real effort to stay off alcohol. Tommy, in particular, had been dry for a couple of months. But it was difficult to stay off wine, while living in a community where one's friends were still drinking. There were also teenagers, living in the house in Winetavern Street who, it was felt, would benefit from a more structured atmosphere. Rita, Ray and some other workers began to attend regular meetings with Ian and Dermot, during which the plans for the move to the Quays were discussed.

No 9 was to be a dry house; Dermot was to live there as house leader on a salary of £15.00 a week (the average industrial wage in 1971 was £20.64 a week). As the ordinary workers were only receiving £2.50 a week this proposal had to be ironed out at committee level, where it met with some resistance. Finally, it was accepted that Dermot was coming in as a professional, and it seemed reasonable that part of the Eastern Health Board grant (£1,500 in 1972) which Simon had been receiving since 1971, under Section 65 of the Health Act 1953, should be used in this way.

Dermot and Ian, in consultation with the workers, were to invite residents whom they thought were ready to join the dry community. Life in No 9 was to be structured around daily breakfast meetings, at which the day's business could be planned, and group therapy meetings three or four times a week, where Ian and Dermot would be the facilitators. It was hoped that residents would be encouraged to discuss their personal problems and any difficulties they might have in living in the community.

No 10 was to be a 'wet house' and night-shelter combined. There would be a 'wet' community living there, much as there had been in Winetavern Street; provision would also be made for a certain number of casual callers. This house was to have its own full-time workers. It was never at any stage considered ideal that these two communities should be living side by side, but at the time Simon had no option. They had to vacate the premises in Winetavern Street, which were needed by the Franciscans, who no doubt regretted their generosity on many occasions during the course of 1970, not least when the bannisters were burnt as firewood!

The actual move occurred in stages. No 9 was being used as a store for a little while and Ray and Rita were stationed there. Tommy was still on the dry and they asked him to come down as a kind of watchman, as kids were breaking in and stealing building materials and the like. At first he enjoyed the job, but he could not cope with being left on his own for too long. On one occasion he got very angry, because the workers had been out somewhere. When they came back he cut his throat in front of them and had to be rushed away to hospital. He went to St Brendan's Psychiatric Hospital for a short period then. Around this time, and partly on account of Tommy's regression, both Ray and Rita resigned from full-time work. This was a great disappointment to Dermot, as he had been relying on their involvement in the setting up of the 'dry' house. In January 1971 everyone moved from Winetavern Street into No 9 Sarsfield Quay, as there was still no water or electricity in No 10. This was a further frustration for those who were to be involved in the 'dry' house. Eventually, however, the renovations were completed and the residents and workers were divided between the two houses.

To grow is to change

The soup-run began to operate from the kitchen of No 10, and administration was centred in an office in Baggot Street, which had been lent by Frank Sweeney. The rapid turnover of full-time workers was becoming a source of worry to the committee. Frank Sweeney told me that his main concern, at this time and later, was the welfare of the workers. It was all too easy in an organisation like Simon to come in full of enthusiasm, work too hard, get emotionally involved, and eventually leave exhausted. The committee felt that this was not good enough.

It was decided that all prospective workers should be assessed; goodwill was not sufficient, the applicant should have some degree of self-knowledge and an ability to cope in extremely stressful situations. The committee also insisted that workers should have forty-eight hours off each week and that this time should be spent away from the houses. To facilitate those who were not from Dublin, it was decided to rent a flat in Dún Laoghaire for this purpose.

Ian Hart, who became a committee member in 1971, felt that the full-time workers would benefit from weekly group sessions in which they could explore their feelings about each other and the residents. He and Dermot McMahon acted as facilitators at these group meetings which were known as 'sensitivity sessions'. Workers attended them voluntarily and, where possible, they were held in a venue away from the houses. Coping with violence was a topic which was frequently raised at sensitivity sessions, as was the difficulty of dealing with the constant verbal aggression. These measures helped to ensure that Simon full-time workers did not strain themselves beyond endurance point.

Meanwhile conflict had arisen over matters of policy. Some members of the committee were seriously concerned about the presence of young able-bodied men in Sarsfield Quay. Simon in Dublin had set out to work with those at the bottom of the pile; its purpose was not to rehabilitate them, in the strict sense of that word, but to provide food, clothing, shelter and a friendly atmosphere in which life might become more meaningful. To use this kind of approach with older men and women was one thing; to encourage young people into a downward spiral was another.

The committee decided that those under forty should no longer be allowed to use Simon, even on a casual basis. This policy was not in fact implemented for many years; successive generations of workers could not find it in their hearts to turn young people away from the door. As a matter of principle, however, it caused conflict early in 1971, and as a result Jock Maguire and Andy Cooper left. They went on to set up Shelter Referral, in the railway building at Merrion Gates, where they lived with a small group of down-and-outs, some of whom had been barred from Simon because of violence; this venture proved to be very successful. They began to collect bottles of all kinds, which they got the men to sort and break before they were sent off for recycling. This idea of a work project was something that Simon was to struggle with for years, before finally getting its own venture off the ground.

There was a new flush of enthusiasm in Simon, when the two houses in Sarsfield Quay started to function as the 'wet house' and the 'dry house'. There were about ten residents in No 9, together with four workers, including Dermot, who lived on the premises. The house was run on democratic lines; the system of meetings allowed ample opportunity for the residents to air their grievances, which they did vociferously on occasion. There was also provision made for a 'crisis meeting', which could be called by anyone at any time. This was to ensure that a serious problem could be dealt with as soon as it arose. Workers and residents together were involved in the running of the house and the organisation of the daily chores. Martin and Betty, a married couple, reigned supreme in the kitchen – other residents were involved in cleaning, doing the laundry, going to the markets for food. One problem at this stage was, in fact, a lack of activities.

Those who were living in No 9 had opted for the three basic rules of the house – no drink, no drugs and no violence. There was an unusual mixture of people there. On the one hand there were the wine drinkers, who when sober were entirely rational and participated well. Then there were a few really eccentric people who tended to be very withdrawn and found it difficult to form any kind of relationship. Finally there were a few young people in their late teens with personality disorders, who had been allowed to stay on in Simon because of extenuating circumstances. Peter, a seventeen year old, stayed because his mother was in the 'wet' house. With such a combination of people, many of whom were making almost superhuman efforts to stay off drink or drugs and were bored as a result, the atmosphere in No 9 tended to be tense and explosive.

No 10, on the other hand, was a more relaxed, if a more

violent, house. Here the 'wet' community lived happily and boisterously. The workers did most of the practical chores – residents helped if they were in the mood. Workers in No 9 envied the easy atmosphere of the 'wet' house, where everything did not have to be dealt with therapeutically, and often stole into the kitchen of No 10 to sit by the fire for half an hour, drinking strong sweet tea, and enjoying the crack. 'Wet' house workers wondered if their No 9 counterparts ever did any 'work', they just seemed to hang around talking to people all day. Even in voluntary organisations, productivity tends to be assessed!

The 'dry' house had a honeymoon of about two months. Then the strain became too great. One by one, those with a drink problem began to drink. A crisis had to be faced; people had to be barred. Some individuals, like Tommy, decided to return to the 'wet' community.

Throughout this period, Ian visited No 9 four times a week to attend therapy groups of about one-and-a-half hours duration. He remained calm and even humorous in the face of all kinds of unusual occurrences. On one occasion, in the course of a group meeting which was being held in the sitting room on the first floor of No 9, bricks came flying through the windows, having been both well aimed and well timed by a couple of angry residents, who had been barred for breaking the drink rule. Ian and Dermot simply organised a retreat to a room at the back of the house where the meeting continued; a good deal of time was spent exploring the feelings of fear and annoyance which had been generated by the incident.

Despite the optimism and enthusiasm, the workers in both houses were operating under intense strain. They were feeling their way and had to cope with all the little disappointments along the road. Verbal aggression was the order of the day in both houses but physical violence continued to lurk in the shadows, particularly in No 10. It came to a head in November 1971. Dermot McMahon describes the scene and how it was coped with.

> . . . a group of four residents forcibly ejected the workers in No. 10 and proceeded to smash up the house. They threw a bed from one of the top windows, damaging a car

parked below. By the time the Guards arrived, they had caused £400 worth of damage. The four individuals were arrested but for some reason they were not charged but released within two hours. For the next four days and nights, they besieged both houses and made it practically impossible for anyone to enter or leave. We considered bringing charges against the people concerned, but refrained from doing so because we felt that we had to protect the confidence and trust which existed between workers and residents. If we were forced into a position of colluding with the police then the concept of an independent therapeutic community would fade and Simon would become just another establishment-type institution which would reject anyone who did not conform to its norms. Of course it would have been much easier if we had charged the troublemakers and had them imprisoned. Very few people would have criticised our action. We were determined not to be intimidated or overwhelmed by violence, and we succeeded in preventing the destruction of the community by unifying and mobilizing the combined resources of the workers and residents.

An indication of this togetherness may be seen in the incidents which followed. Due to the amount of damage suffered by No. 10 it became necessary to limit the number of people staying there and we made arrangements to accommodate the surplus in other city hostels. The workers drew up a list of people who they felt could be accommodated elsewhere for the time being and included in this list were certain residents who were very troublesome and unco-operative. Normally we could cope with these people but at this point in time we needed help and co-operation if Simon was to continue functioning. We called a meeting of both houses and explained the situation to the residents. We went through the list name by name and discussed each person and then voted whether he or she should stay. It was gratifying to see the residents taking an active part in the decision-making which affected their lives. They were as concerned as ourselves that Simon should continue to function. It is true to say that we workers could not have kept the houses open without the help and support of the residents. That November episode had the effect of bringing

everyone much closer together, and it proved to be an important learning experience for all concerned. The group laying siege to the house finally exhausted itself, and gradually they drifted away. We had proved that there are ways of coping with violence other than resorting to counter-violence or repression. We could have squashed the opposition if we had decided to use the forces of law and order but instead we confronted violence with caring, understanding and common sense, and by harnessing our combined resources.
(*A Group Approach to Socially Deprived People*, Dublin, Runa, 1975, pp 17, 18)

In January, 1972, Simon acquired additional premises at No 42 Harcourt Street under a caretaker's agreement with a property developer. The soup-run immediately started to use the basement of this house as its headquarters. Another office was also needed, as the room in Baggot Street was no longer available. The house in Harcourt Street quickly became a multi-purpose building. Administration operated from the first floor, old clothes and furniture were stored at ground level. Dermot McMahon decided to live in the Harcourt Street house, while still working a full day on the quays. In the following months some other workers followed suit. Living on the quays for more than a year proved almost impossible; those who were involved in the ever-increasing work of administration were happy to live in a less tense atmosphere.

Nos 9 and 10 continued to function well, despite a number of problems related mainly to a shortage of workers. The 'dry' house and 'wet' house structure remained intact, but the rigour of the therapeutic community idea had been somewhat modified. Ian continued to attend group sessions, and he built up successful relationships with some of the residents.

In the autumn of 1972 the Irish Life Assurance Company gave Simon a small house in Northumberland Square, off Abbey Street, on a caretaker's agreement. This proved a god-send, as it allowed four of the No 9 residents, who needed a quiet atmosphere, to establish a little 'home' for themselves, with the aid of one worker. By this time, Simon had gathered momentum; it had a high profile in the media, and was being funded almost entirely by the general public. Having come a long way from its origins as a part-time student organisation, it had not only put down its roots, but had begun to spread its branches.

3

I'M A HUMAN BEING LIKE YOURSELF

Homelessness – a condition not to be envied

> Who are the homeless? Do you really know? Have you ever, even for one day, alone or with your family, been entirely without a home, without a place of your own, dependent on friends, on relatives, or on some strange, overcrowded, vaguely threatening hostel for a night's sleep? Have you ever slept out – not from choice, but simply because you had no place to go? . . . Unless you *have* actually experienced the shock of finding yourself without a roof you can call your own, the odds are that you do not really *know* who the homeless are, or what homelessness really means.

For most of us, the answer to the question, so starkly posed by Anton Wallich-Clifford (*No Fixed Abode*, London, Macmillan, 1974, p. 11) would be a definite 'No'; and that is as it should be. Home is somewhere we tend to take for granted – a kind of cocoon, or protective environment, where we can relax and be nourished when we are weary. Home is also a place into which we put energy, so that it will meet our needs and be an expression of our personal taste. Children like to go home after a hard day at school. Invalids long to come home from hospital. Parents create a home for each other and for their children. There is an excitement also in moving away from the family home, either as an individual or as a couple, in order to create a new home. It can be fun to decorate the room or the flat to one's own taste, and to know that here one can have privacy and the freedom to entertain friends. Sometimes we even talk about feeling 'at home' somewhere else, perhaps in a friend's house. Nowadays many people wonder if perhaps it would be wiser for births and deaths to occur in the familiar, non-threatening environment of the home. All this would seem to suggest that a home is more than simply a roof over one's head.

Mr Fred Donohue, Director of Community Care in the Eastern Health Board Region, addressed the 1978 Simon National Conference on the subject of 'The Homeless Person and the Community', and said:

> Homelessness does not alone mean the absence of a roof; it means the absence of all the other things that we associate with home; a place that is ours where we are free from being pushed around, where there is love, where there is affection, and where we, too, can express our affection. If these things are missing, if a person is homeless or hungry, then those concepts which the rest of the community proclaim so loudly: justice, freedom, the rights to private property and so on are all ephemeral and distant concepts to be discussed by lawyers and jurists. They have little relevance to the person who is hungry and has not got a home.
>
> (*Simon Ireland Newsletter*, April, 1978)

Homelessness is, of course, related to lack of adequate housing. In a society like ours, the high cost of housing, coupled with the unequal distribution of income, has meant that many people, whether those in poorly paid employment or those reliant on social welfare, have been unable to meet the full economic cost of accommodation of a reasonable standard. Those who hope to buy a house with the help of a mortgage must have a good income and secure employment. Finding decent accommodation in the private rented sector also necessitates a good income; much substandard housing exists in this sector, and often the poor are the ones who are exploited.

Housing in Ireland was almost entirely left to private developers and landlords until the 1930s, with the beginning of a modest public housing programme. But the financing of public housing was uneven, permitting the construction of a greater number of houses a year in the early 1950s and in the mid-1970s than at other times. In the mid-1980s about 6,000 local authority houses were being built each year.

No scientific attempts were made to study special categories in need until a report on the Irish Housing System published by The Economic and Social Research Institute in 1979 suggested that a wide range of serious housing problems still persisted and affected significant numbers of Ireland's population. In August 1981, there were more than 8,000 on the waiting list for local authority housing in the Dublin area alone; Dublin Corporation had plans to complete only 1,500 dwellings in the period 1981/1982. Those on the waiting list were either family units or elderly people. Only those in extremely grave housing circumstances had any chance of being housed; single people under the age of 50 were not considered at all except on special medical grounds.

Because there was no specific reference to the single homeless in our legislation, Dr John O'Connell, TD in May 1978 submitted a written parliamentary question to the then Minister for Health, Mr Charles Haughey, asking who was responsible for the provision of services for homeless people. Mr Haughey's reply, which referred to section 54 of the Health Act 1953, brought to light the fact that a single homeless person had no statutory right to a home. All he or she was entitled to was shelter or accommodation in a County Home or a hostel (*Simon Ireland Newsletter*, May, 1978). Earlier that year, Ercus Stewart, a practising barrister, had pointed out that:

> the Constitution, itself, which is superior to all ordinary laws, gives to private property rights far greater protection than it does to an individual citizen's rights to a home . . . .
> (*Simon Ireland Newsletter*, March, 1978)

So it should hardly come as a surprise that we now have in Irish society a group of 'single homeless' who are without a settled way of life. Justin O'Brien, writing on the subject of 'Poverty and Homelessness', attempted to describe this alienated group:

> They have more often been described as vagrants, vagabonds, tramps, down and outs, dossers, skid row people, destitutes – all names which imply stigma and prejudice and deny a central feature of their condition, namely, being homeless. As a group they are usually readily identifiable in the public consciousness and are publicly visible by reason of their poor clothing and attire, their unkempt

> appearance and perhaps by the committal of anti-social acts such as begging and drunkenness, attracting a mixture of sympathy, indignation and rejection from the public. They are one of the most obvious examples of the existence of poverty and destitution in Irish society, despite its growing prosperity and the expansion of the State's Welfare and Social Services.
> (*One Million Poor*, ed. Stanislaus Kennedy, Dublin, Turoe Press, 1981, p. 76)

It is difficult to move beyond the point of seeing homelessness as an intractable problem and the single homeless as a hopeless problem group. Recently, however, researchers have become interested in looking at homelessness through the eyes of the so-called 'dosser'. This approach allows us to see the 'dosser' as a human being like ourselves, with hopes and fears, memories and aspirations. All too often, as we plough through the ever-increasing mire of statistics, we become befuddled and miss this vital element. Perhaps an understanding of our common humanity can empower us as a society to identify truthfully the real causes of homelessness and to tackle them courageously. But we cannot do this unless we learn to listen to the stories of those who find themselves, for a multitude of reasons, living on skid row.

I've been there and back

The *Irish Press*, of Monday, December 11, 1972, carried Archie Hill's story of his journey through skid row. Archie is an Englishman, and his references are to the English prison and welfare systems; nevertheless, much of what he has to say would be equally applicable to the Irish situation. He was born in 1926, one of a family of ten:

> 'There was no family unity or harmony, only a fight for survival amid the debris of an alcoholic father and a highly neurotic mother. I think I started to fight the world from the first day I stood on my own two feet. Some people ought not to have children and my mother and father were among these. My father was ever in and out of prison. When other boys sneered, mocked or laughed at this, I would fight them. Once I pinned a boy's hand to a wheelbarrow with the prong of a garden fork. I earned the

reputation, "Like father, like son", and became known as a thug and a tearaway.

'Eventually I learned how to use the reputation as armour to keep the world away from me. Ambivalence is cancer of the soul. If you love-hate your parents there is a lot of guilt. You'll wish your father dead, and that you were instrumental in killing him, and there's this terrible pressure of guilt to live with.

'I left home at 18 after a fight with my father, served in the R.A.F. for six years, then joined the civil police. During my R.A.F. years I'd been drinking heavily. In the Middle East alcohol was cheap and potent. Now, as a civil policeman, I needed large amounts of whiskey to keep me functioning. I was found sleeping it off in a car park one night and was sacked. Being fired from the police was my first great loss through alcohol, but even so my drinking increased. My wife left me, eventually divorced me, and after an attempt at suicide I was committed to a mental hospital.'

Archie was in and out of mental hospitals over the next few years and eventually had to serve a two year prison sentence for stealing food and methylated spirits.

'It is 16 years now since I first came to London. I arrived in the "Big City" hard on the heels of the prison discharge. I'd gone home first to my mother's house. It was raining. I was wet and cold. I knocked on the door and my mother called, "Who is it?"

'And I answered, "It's me, it's Archie."

'I pleaded to be let in but her words were nails hammering the door of the world shut.

' "Get away from here," she said, "you're not wanted."

'I walked back down the wet street and had more hate in me than is sane to carry. I went to London with a turned-up jacket collar and no overcoat, and less than a shilling in my pocket. I hung about Waterloo Station and chummed up with a homeless scouse who begged enough money for us both to get drunk on scrumpy cider. This was the beginning of my life on Skid Row.

'It was here that I learned that hypocrisy bows to the stars while it spits on a tramp, and that the world has many hypocrites. It was here that I learned that society has more dinners than appetite, but will not share its surplus. It was here that I learned that far too many people put Christianity on a pedestal instead of into circulation. On bomb-sites, wastelands, in decayed and crumbling houses. These were home. Sometimes I lived alone, other times with groups that quarrelled and argued and fought and dwelt in regions of private madness. Sometimes I cared about the loneliness, other times I didn't. It was all a matter of degree, it all depended on how much the day had gnawed at me, it all depended on how much drink I'd got in my belly and bottle.

'No one elects to live on Skid Row. It is not a place, it is a condition – a condition which overtakes you. One homeless night merges with another, and another, until evidence of one's physical deterioration is but a mirror of one's spiritual collapse. Each day on Skid Row makes the dual condition worse. You need a bath, a shave, a toothbrush. You need those little things which loom so large in absence. It is NOW that the Welfare and Church workers are needed; not at night when you're sprawled around a bonfire with alcohol in your system to keep the world at bay.

'We were – and are – ugly to look at, we were unclean and vile and smelly, and our instincts erupted into violent anger if we were interfered with. We were no part of society. We had no part of ourselves to give, we were in a permanent prison of self and circumstance. We were – and are – zoological specimens, the toys of the welfare bodies, prison-residue, the policeman's bread and butter. We were emptiness, we were nothing; we were – and are – the story of men who have no present or future; no plans, no promise of better things to come, no hearth, no home, no love, no laughter, no pity to give or take, no honour, no self-respect. Horizons are so small at the world's end . . . .

'The weeks and months went by, winter into summer; and one day I looked at my companions and felt sober terror welling up inside me. I had to get away – even if it meant going back to prison, I had to get away. In the centre of my life a sober streak stood aghast and stared out at the dying men and women who shared my existence. A whimper started deep inside my thoughts, a whimper of protest which swelled and exploded into a vast silent "NO". I had to get away. I had to get away and find myself and find the world I'd come from, if it were still there. O Christ, I hoped – let it still be there. I needed to clean up and go back into the world, no matter how hostile. I needed a job and a place to live; I needed a start. First of all I tried a Discharged Prisoners' Aid Society, but there was no help forthcoming. I went to a religion-orientated hostel, but couldn't get a place because I didn't have enough money for my bed and keep.

'I went to the National Assistance Board, but was told that I couldn't get an allowance until I had an address. I explained that I couldn't get an address unless I had money. I walked away from that place sneering at the littleness of God. I longed for the oblivion of alcohol. But some protective stubbornness inside me would not let me unstopper the "jake" bottle in my pocket. I walked several miles to a Women's Voluntary Service place. Their eyes clouded over when they saw me, and under the dirt I felt my face flush with shame. But they were conscious of my need and not my misdemeanours; they piled clothing into my eager hands. I mumbled and stumbled my thanks, then went and found a public lavatory for a locked door's pennyworth so that I could change from the rags I was wearing. When I emerged I felt newborn, despite the fact that the new clothes were miles too big for me. I went to Waterloo Station, the methys' haunting ground. Down in the wash-place an Irishman was having a shave. I begged a loan of his razor, and scraped away my beard with the luxury of good soap and sharp steel. I saw the lower part of my face stand out white as a girl's neck. The top part was weather brown and the drink lines in my face made me look about 50. My teeth were yellow with neglect, and I promised them a toothbrush at the first opportunity. I washed the razor carefully and gave it back to the Irishman. He came after me as I went up the steps, put a hand on my shoulder and then put ten shillings in my hand.

"Good luck," he said, "and God bless."

'I could have wept. With the ten shillings, I booked in at a hostel. Next morning I'd got an address for the National Assistance Board, so I could get financial help. That was my good-bye to Skid Row. Not that I was finished with it – I merely stopped living there.

'That was all a good many years ago. My world now is good and clean and on axis. But I still go back to the waste-lands, the empty houses, the railway stations and the decaying warrens where men and women still exist. During the past eight years I think I've been responsible for influencing three such lives to come out of the mess.'

Alone in an alien world

Archie says that no one chooses to live on skid row, defining it not as a place but as a condition – a condition which over-takes somebody. Ian Hart's research into the backgrounds of those people with whom Dublin Simon has been involved supports this view. People have become homeless for a wide variety of reasons. Many of them:

> ... had had miserable lives through little fault of their own. Most had been born in poverty, among large families beset by heavy drinking and quarrelling ... a notable proportion had spent some part of their childhood in institutions. Others had contracted disastrous marriages which had broken up after much conflict. In 8 per cent of cases the death of a parent or spouse preceded a person's decline into skid row.
> (*Dublin Simon Community: An Exploration*, Dublin, ESRI, 1978, p. 23)

This last statistic is an important one to consider because it brings up the idea of a precipitating factor in the downward spiral. Most people go through difficult times in their lives; they have to face illness or unemployment or a bereavement, or they may suffer from depression or other forms of emo-tional disturbance. But most people pull through; they do not lose home and family and everything they cherish. For those who do not weather the crises of life, there is usually a turning-point – a time when they might have taken either of two roads, and they take the downward path. I am not suggest-ing that they choose it; they drift into it because there is not enough support from family, friends or the social services to do anything else. Once they start to live in this other world –

outside society – it becomes increasingly difficult to return. Ian Hart suggests (*op. cit.*, pp. 23, 24) that someone who, because of a disastrous past, lacks a sense of meaning in life needs enormous personal courage if he or she is to cope with life creatively.

Perhaps the most crucial element in the makeup of those who have become homeless is the fact that they are usually incapable of forming and sustaining meaningful friendships. Archie pointed out that early on he learned to keep the world away from him. But this kind of defence mechanism can have disastrous results; without confidence in relationships with others it is impossible to establish a sense of personal identity. One long-term Simon co-worker told me that she thought of Simon work as 'befriending the homeless'. This brings to mind again the idea of 'home'. No more than skid row, home is not just a place; it is a condition and one we take for granted. Having a 'home' is not simply about ownership; it is also about *feeling* 'at home' in the world, among other people. The homeless person does not have this sense of belonging. He or she must re-learn to love and to trust. Marie Lynch, who worked for a period in Dublin Simon, did a thesis on 'The Dublin Dosser'; in her recommendations regarding rehabilitation she sees the dosser as:

> . . . essentially one who has not been affirmed. His behaviour betrays a contempt for society and an imbalance in adjusting to circumstances. In order to be affirmed he must learn, again and again, that he is loved.
> (Thesis for MSc in Applied Social Studies, 1975, New University of Ulster)

A night on the soup-run

The Dublin Simon Community has been in existence now for over eighteen years, but there are still people sleeping rough. Many of them are loners, who would not wish to live in the Simon Shelter or in one of the residential houses. Community living is not for everybody. Others are newcomers to skid row, perhaps young people who have just left home. Miriam McCarthy visits many of these on a weekly basis, sometimes more often. She is in constant contact with the soup-run, which goes out each night to visit the 'regulars', and also keeps an eye out for anyone new on the scene. A major feature of the soup-run is its consistency. The people know that every night without fail, whatever the weather, Simon will come. The world has become a little more 'homely'. There are people who can be relied upon.

One Monday evening in late February 1983, I set out reluctantly for the Simon house in Sean MacDermott Street, from which the soup-run operated. Though dry, it was bitterly cold, and I felt cheated out of my normal Monday evening routine – a few hours by the fire with a good book, and an early night. It was 9.30 pm when I arrived. 35 Sean MacDermott Street is a large residential Simon house, the basement of which has been used as the headquarters for the soup-run since 1980. I went down the outdoor metal stairs, through a hall which was full of blankets, and found myself in a spacious, well-equipped soup-kitchen; a number of the soup-runners had already arrived and were busy cooking soup in large pots over the gas, or making up meat and cheese sandwiches. Gradually others trickled in until there were nine in all – four men and five women. Most of them were in their twenties, but Pat Walsh, who was acting as co-ordinator for the night, was a middle-aged man. He told me that he had been doing the Monday night soup-run for ten years; having seen a Simon advertisement in the paper in 1972, asking desperately for car owners to help on the soup-run, he decided to offer his services. He has not been involved in any other aspect of Simon; he does not have time to attend meetings or conferences, but he is happy to maintain his commitment to the Monday night run.

Besides the kitchen equipment, which included a fridge, the room contained a long rack on which hung a selection of clothing. Sometimes those being visited needed shoes, clothes or blankets as well as food. Each evening before setting out, the soup-runners read the report, which has been written up by the previous night's volunteers. Thus they discover if any of the 'regulars' need anything special; the report would also mention if any new people had been located. There was a friendly atmosphere among the volunteers as they prepared for their task.

The old-timers guided the newer recruits and answered many of my questions. About half of those present had been on the job for two years or more; some of the others were quite new. On this particular evening, the soup-runners were very annoyed because their Sunday night counterparts had left the kitchen in a mess – and this had not been the first time! A strongly worded notice was composed and left prominently on the notice-board, in the hope that consciences would be pricked and a sparkling kitchen would await them the following week.

When the preparations had been completed, the plan for the night was drawn up. There were three cars. This meant that three groups could go out, each doing a different run. Specific routes were decided upon – north side, south side and city centre; the list of regulars was divided out.

As we headed up the stairs to the street armed with flasks of soup and packets of sandwiches, someone shouted:

'Oh, the eggs.'

I was mystified, until I discovered that certain people liked to get a hard-boiled egg as well as some sandwiches – and of course it would be a valuable protein addition to the diet of someone sleeping rough. I travelled with Pat and a girl called Eileen, a soup-runner of five years standing who works in the civil service. She and Pat had worked together before and they both knew the ropes. We were on the southside run and we headed off through the back streets towards Ringsend.

'We're going first to the Dump,' Pat told me, 'to see a man who was living in appalling conditions when we first discovered him. He had a low lean-to, made from corrugated tin and tarpaulin. One night he had a heart attack; luckily we found him and got him an ambulance. When we got him out of the lean-to that time, it more or less collapsed. He was in hospital for quite some time. When he came out, Simon had a hut ready for him on the exact spot of his old home.'

By this time we had arrived at the Dump. Pat parked the car; Eileen took a couple of eggs, some sandwiches and a flask, and armed with a torch, we set out to visit Jack. We walked a good quarter of a mile over very rough terrain which would have been quite treacherous without the friendly beam of the torch. Separated from Sandymount beach on our right by a stretch of water which made us even chillier, we could see the lights forming their fairy patterns round the bay; but on our left stretched the Dump, a godforsaken patch of waste ground.

I wondered why anyone would choose this place to create a home. Having turned our backs to the sea, we climbed a little, and finally reached Jack's hut.

Pat knocks at the door.

'Are you awake, Jack, it's Simon.'

The door opens.

'Good night to you. Is it cold out to-night?' Jack asks us politely.

He is sitting up in bed, wearing a big overcoat on top of his other clothes, a weather-beaten man with piercing eyes.

'It is cold,' Eileen replies. 'How are you? Would you like some soup?'

'Yes,' he responds, 'the saucepan is over there, it is nice and clean.'

While Eileen pours some soup into his saucepan, he eats one of the hard-boiled eggs. Then he drinks his soup while he chats to us. He has a transistor radio, one of his most prized possessions. According to the news reports this evening there is snow in Kilkenny and the RTE announcers are complaining about their salaries. Jack feels that because of the recession not enough money is available to RTE; as a result the quality of the programmes has deteriorated.

'I feel quite disgruntled about it all. And as for Radio Nova, that's all pop – all right for the youngsters I suppose.'

Having finished the soup, he puts the saucepan back on the shelf. Another egg and a couple of sandwiches go beside it for the morning. He accepts a few cigarettes and then expresses concern about us standing in the cold.

'I won't detain you any longer, now,' he says.

We say goodnight. He closes his door and fastens it up with a bit of rope. As we walked back to the car Pat told me that little was known about Jack. He did not have a drink problem, was originally from Wicklow and had spent some years in Canada.

Next we visited Marty, who has a hut on a more accessible part of the dump. He was asleep so Eileen left some sandwiches and an egg. The soup-runners do not like to waken people who have really settled in for the night, as once they are warm they do not wish to be disturbed. The situation was the same with the next man we visited – John Joe Higgins at Merrion Gates. Again Eileen left sandwiches and cigarettes.

Our next stop was further out on Merrion Road, where we visited a youngish man, Tommy, who was living in a make-shift tent-cum-hut on the green patch opposite Blackrock College. He was sitting at a fire trying to keep warm; despite a home-made chimney in the canvas, it was very smoky inside. Pat went in and chatted to him for a few minutes; he accepted the soup and sandwiches and said he needed nothing else.

On our way back towards town we stopped at a church where one 'regular', Jimmy, sleeps in the side porch. A lean man in his thirties with dull eyes, Jimmy was not on for talk. He would have liked tomato soup but we only had scotch broth. Jimmy had been lying in one corner of the porch, covered with coats. There was another figure in the shadows on the opposite side. He grunted, did not seem to show any interest in the soup. Pat suspected that he was warm, being well covered, and that he did not wish to be disturbed. Getting warm is quite a process for someone who sleeps rough in Ireland in February.

On our way back towards town Eileen and Pat told me about Jane. Simon has known her since the early days, a chubby little lady with red cheeks and sparkling eyes, who always carries six or seven plastic carrier bags. For many years she used to sleep rough over on the north side in the general vicinity of the Richmond Hospital. For one longish period, Frank Duff's porch was her home. She seemed to have absolutely no desire to move indoors. It was obvious to the early soup-runners that a Simon house was not the answer for Jane, but for a long time the volunteers felt that if she had some kind of flat she could use it as she wished.

Jane spends the early morning around the churches, praying and resting. And then she walks, often for miles. Sandymount Strand is a favourite haunt and seems to have particular memories for her. Perhaps she was in service there once. It appears that she was married and had a daughter. However, she seems to have lost all connection with family, and at some point she drifted into her present way of life. She has been known to talk at length about Sandymount, speaking poetically of white horses riding on the sea. Finally the volunteers got her to accept the idea of a flat; it is in a deserted corporation block in Halston Street – nice and central. She does not go to bed there, but does spend from about 1.00 am to 6.00 am sitting in a chair dozing, or just pottering around. She continues to wander around during the day with her carrier bags.

Each night, sometime after midnight, the soup-runners pick her up in the lobby of Holles Street Hospital, her last port of call. She was glad to see us when we arrived and enjoyed sitting, chatting, in the front seat of the car. She wondered what we were all giving up for Lent. She was going off the sweets herself. We drove across the Liffey and turned to the left at the top of O'Connell Street; then Pat stopped outside a chipper near her Halston Street flat and Eileen asked:

'The usual, Jane, is it?'

Jane nodded. 'The usual' was a single and a bunburger which she would enjoy back in her flat, with a little of the Simon soup. When Eileen returned we headed for the flat. We went in with Jane and stayed chatting for about ten minutes. She is alone in this big old barracks of a place, but that does not seem to bother her. The flat is a bit chaotic, like her plastic bags. She saves every scrap of paper or bread or whatever in case she might hit hard times. When we leave she comes down and waves to us from the steps of the building, a tiny, eccentric figure, framed by the massive wooden door.

We return to the car. Pat and Eileen are very fond of Jane. They enjoy meeting her and are happy that she has a roof over her head for a few hours of the night. We return to the soup kitchen in Sean MacDermott Street, where a wash-up operation is already in progress. The soup-runners are tired now, but still anxious to hear the news from the other routes. A representative from each of the groups fills in the report, which will be the continuity link for the Tuesday night team. When all is shipshape the soup kitchen is locked and everyone heads for home. As we drive off through the deserted city streets, Pat explains that the volunteers see that everyone has a lift home. He drops me off at 1.30 am. He heads then for Rathmines with Eileen before returning to his own home on the northside.

If I'd accepted that, I might have been a better man today . . . The soup-run visits John Joe Higgins, but more often than not he is asleep at that time of the night. Although he was one of the first residents in Winetavern Street, he now lives near the sea in a little corrugated iron hut, with an orange plastic roof. I decided to visit him. Having been told that he often begged outside his local church, I wasn't surprised to find him there one Tuesday shortly after midday. He said he would be happy to have a chat with me, but he didn't want to miss his 'regulars' from twelve o'clock Mass. He gave me his key and told me to go on ahead and make myself 'at home'. He would come along as soon as he was ready. I left him – a tall, stately man, with a warm smile and gentle eyes.

John Joe's hut is situated beside a wall near a level crossing. As well as the hut itself, he uses a little walled-in corner as a cooking and sitting area. He has this cordoned off by means of a long leatherette sofa and he often has flowers in jamjars at the entrance to his patio-style living area. The day was clear and crisp, one of the better March days. The sun was shining and the sea was blue. John Joe had his vegetables arranged on a little raised wall which serves as a shelf; beside them were his cooking utensils, a water container and some lovely shells. There was plenty of wood in the corner; on fine days he lights a fire.

I opened the padlock with the key and looked into the hut. A certain amount of light shone through the orange plastic roof. Inside was a matress well raised off the floor; around the sides of the hut were wooden shelves neatly lined with clean newspapers. There were plenty of blankets on the bed, a pair of socks hanging up to dry, a jacket on a clothes hanger, and on the shelves a toothbrush, a clothes brush, shoe polish, shaving gear, a towel, and a little crucifix. The place was spick and span – not surprising when one considers that it is the home of an ex-army man.

I sat down on a little chair inside the hut for ten minutes or so. Then John Joe arrived with a kettle of boiling water which the signal men at the station had given to him.

'They never see me stuck for the water for a shave or a cup of bovril,' he told me. 'They're great people, the signal men, and as for the people who live around here, they're some of the best. And they're very good to me. Be sure to say that in the book, too.'

There is limited space in the hut. I stand up to let John

Joe pass. He decides to sit into the bed. But first he makes two cups of bovril and passes one of them to me. I sit down again on my chair. John Joe is anxious about my comfort. We settle down and begin to sip our bovril. Then he starts to tell me his story.

He was born in 1917 and lived in Watling Street, facing Guinness's Brewery, where, according to himself, he first got the smell of the stout. His father was abroad in the army, so he lived with his mother's people. It was a busy house with the grandparents living there and other children. John Joe had only one sister, but there were cousins as well – and Aunt Kate, who seemed to be quite a formidable woman.

'My mother died when I was only a toddler, about three year old – and I remember well, I tried to climb into the coffin', John Joe told me. 'My aunt Kate brought me up, but I was the wild one of the house. In 1927 I got sent to Artane and I'll tell you how it happened. You might think it is a bit peculiar, but in them days things were rough. People weren't very rich and it was a bit of a struggle. One day I was on a message up to Patrick Street. I was given two shillings and I was to get a sack of loaves – you'd get twelve or fourteen loaves of bread for that and there were nine in our family in Watling Street. Well, what did I do with the two shillings only spend it buying cakes. I wasn't even nine, then. I was caught and my aunt gave me a box on the ear and brought me over to the District Court and so I got sent to Artane.

'Them were the hard days. It was tough and rough there and you didn't get very much food. I was always hungry. The place was open, but very few ran away. I'll tell you why. If you ran away and got caught, you were sent out into the yard before all the others at play time – the offender you were called – and the brothers gave the other lads instructions to kick you and beat you up. That was allowed. It was a very strict school. But they gave you a trade, I'll say that for them. My trade was Ladies' and Gents' Tailoring. It was all handwork. I used to do the basting out, and put fur collars on ladies' coats and make buttonholes by hand.

'In 1934 I got a job and came home. I was sixteen years of age – young, spruce, and as fit as a fiddle. The job was in Mary's Abbey off Capel Street. It was all handwork and I earned seven shillings and sixpence a week. There were good days and bad days. Sure life has changed now. I suppose the young ones have to have their day. Anyway after a few years I got tired of the job. I wasn't advancing in life at all, only getting worse. I packed it in and went on the Labour. I got ten shillings a week. One week when I got paid I thought to myself – now this is no use to me, this carrying on here, there's no future in it. So when I got the ten bob – that's all I had in my pocket, no smokes, no food – I walked from the city of Dublin out to Dún Laoghaire and I got the boat to Holyhead. The fare was ten shillings. I got off the boat in the early hours of the morning and started walking the roads towards Cheshire. You see, I wanted to get to Liverpool. It was late at night so after a while I lay down on the side of the road and went to sleep – that was my first time ever to sleep out. I was hardy then, but I didn't like it all the same. It was just something I had to do. If you make your bed you have to lie on it. You can't be going around pleading for sympathy off people, because everyone has their own troubles. Life must go on. You meet it as you come to it, and you accept it, you have to do.'

John Joe walked his way through Cheshire and eventually reached Liverpool. There he went into a pub called 'The Dublin Packet', which was owned by Dixie Dean, a soccer player of great repute. He had a few pints there, having tapped (or begged) a few bob in the course of the journey. He stayed for a while in Liverpool, living in hostels and doing casual work. Eventually he decided to make for London.

'I worked in hotels in London, being a great lover of cooking. I can cook, too. When you're looking after yourself, you must do it. I like things boiled rather than fried. Spare ribs and cabbage now, that's a great dinner. And I'd never throw the cabbage water away, I always drink the whole lot. I lived in hostels mostly when I was in London. I worked in the Cumberland Hotel. I started there as a kitchen porter and then became a vegetable cook. Then I worked with a fish cook in another establishment. I was very clean with the food. I was spruce and clean them days. One day the manager called me over and told me that he wanted to send me away to a college to become a chef. I didn't take that opportunity. I had a win on the dogs and went on the rampage. If I'd accepted that, I might have been a better man today. In a way I regret it . . . .

'Then I started to tramp the roads. And I was drinking too much. I just wanted to be free. I didn't want to be tied down. I went from spike to spike – they're the county homes you know. I'd go in and get a bath, like and then I'd be off again. I was all over the British Isles and I enjoyed it. I was free and there was no-one telling me to do this and do that. The reason you'd go in to the spikes is to get cleaned up – a wash and a shave and maybe a change of clothes. Then you'd be off again. You might sit down by the side of the road and make a drum of tea, to your own taste, or you might drop into some field and dig up some spuds. Then in 1938, when I was in Liverpool again, I joined the army. I joined up in Seymour Street and the recruiting officer gave us tickets for food and lodging in the Salvation Army Hostel, just across the road. We were there for three nights, and then I was sent over to Omagh with the Enniskillen Fusiliers. I was there for six months and then I went on to do more training with the regiment in Yorkshire. Then, in 1939, the war broke out.'

John Joe went on to tell me about his experiences during the war. He landed in Boulogne in France and then went south. He described the forced march he was involved in, where for seven days they had to march with full equipment – rifle, ammunition and boots – and they were only given ten minutes resting time every hour. The Germans broke through their ranks during that march. He had great respect for General Rommel and felt that no one should underestimate him as a general. Hitler treated him badly in the end. During the war the fusiliers only received two shillings a day.

In 1945, John Joe got a gratuity of £175 – he drank the lot and returned to tramping the roads. After some years he came back to Ireland. When Simon first came in contact with him in 1969, he was sleeping in the cars in Smithfield. He drank a lot of wine at that time. Having lived in Winetavern Street for a year, he then moved with Simon to Sarsfield Quay. There was a good deal of violence there at that time and John Joe was involved in a lot of it. He and some others were asked to leave at one stage and they went out to live in Shelter Referral at Merrion Gates. I asked him how he felt about Simon – and about life in general.

'They're a good crowd. I'll be going in to see them shortly.

And of course the soup-run visits me. I went back sleeping rough because when you're among a crowd of lads, you can't control the drink. You might stay off it for a while, but you can't control it. I used to be violent, but I've changed. Maybe it is that I'm getting older but when I hear a loud word now I'm off. I'm very happy here – the people in this locality all know me. Simon visits me at night and leaves me sandwiches and cigarettes. I still like a drink, and I wouldn't like to break the rules in the Shelter, or upset other people who are trying to stay off. I only drink the wine now – stout is a waste of time. I wouldn't give wine to a young man, though. I enjoyed Christmas. I had a singsong here with Simon and the people around. It was great altogether. The Simon were very good to me – they helped me up off the street when I didn't need to be there, guided me and helped me and fed me and dressed me and since then I've been making a bit of progress, with their help. It's the best organisation in the world, bar none.'

4

ORDER OR CHAOS?

Putting a shape on things

In the autumn of 1971, there was a major exodus from the full-time worker force on Sarsfield Quay. Among the new recruits was a rather serious young man, who contrary to the custom of the time, did not wear blue jeans and an open-necked shirt. Dick Shannon was tall and slender, with a shock of black hair, which he absent-mindedly pushed out of his eyes from time to time. He dressed in dark suits and wore a shirt and tie. A twenty-one year old, he had spent some years in a religious order and had heard of Simon initially through reading the English Catholic newspapers. Subsequently he met some people who had been involved in the house in Winetavern Street. He liked the sound of the Simon Community, particularly the idea of workers and residents living together. The non-denominational aspect also appealed to him as did the emphasis on campaign on behalf of the rootless. He decided to become a full-time worker and was placed in No 9 Sarsfield Quay, where Dermot McMahon was still house-leader of the therapeutic community project. He experienced no great problem settling in, but the one thing for which he was not prepared was the tremendous barrage of colourful language which often issued forth from the residents. The atmosphere at the time was tense and No 9 was still being run in a very structured fashion.

Almost from the beginning, Dick took an interest in administration. Accounting work was being done voluntarily in an office in Baggot Street; everything else depended on the full-time workers. Dick was aware that correspondence was often neglected. Letters arrived at Sarsfield Quay and were mislaid. Requests from outside groups who required a speaker, were not always followed up. The flag days in 1971 just happened – a few people collected outside the Bank of Ireland in Westmoreland Street. With a little organisation a lot more could have been achieved.

In December 1971 the full-time workers elected Dick to the position of Community Leader with responsibility for co-ordinating the various aspects of the life of the community. This was despite the fact that he had been a worker for only three months. By this stage he had rooted out an old typewriter and was spending a considerable amount of time answering letters in the little, crowded office in No 9. In his new post he was also responsible for the finances of the Community. He it was who dealt with the bank, saw to the payment of full-time workers, and allocated running expenses to the houses.

As the months passed, and the Community began to expand, with the acquisition of the property in Harcourt Street and a house in Northumberland Square (see p. 51), it became obvious that the job of Community Leader was too much for one person. A separate post of Administrator was created and Dick began to work full-time in this capacity from a new office in Harcourt Street. Another full-time worker became Community Leader and assumed responsibility for co-ordinating activities in the houses and among part-time workers.

The moving of the office to 42 Harcourt Street was important. It meant that Committee meetings and full-time worker assessments could be held away from the houses on the quays. This led to a more serious and professional approach. The office in No 9 had contained the only phone which Simon possessed and it rang constantly. A large safe was also kept there; it contained the housekeeping money, various forms of medication needed by the residents and numerous personal belongings left in for safe keeping. During Committee meetings which were held in this tiny room, it was not unusual to have as many as twenty interruptions. It must have been quite off-putting for prospective workers to be interviewed under these conditions. But at the time this all seemed quite acceptable to the Simon workers; in fact some may even have thought it desirable that administration should function amid the chaos of everyday Simon life. For someone like Bob Cashman, an experienced Committee-man, the situation must have been quite frustrating.

Dick Shannon saw the need for administrative order; a precise person himself, he found it difficult to function in such chaos. He not only encouraged the move to Harcourt Street, but insisted that proper minutes should be kept and typed, that an agenda should be sent out in advance to Committee members, and that a file should be opened for press cuttings about Simon.

Fund-raising was becoming a major issue as the Community expanded. The expenditure for the year ending November 1971 was £8,500, of which £1,500 came as a grant from the Eastern Health Board. The figures almost doubled the following year; financial statements show an expenditure of £14,222 for the year ending November 1972. The grant from the Health Board did not increase; the rest of the money came through donations, flag days, carol singing and other fund-raising events.

Late in 1972 Dick saw the need for a fund-raising committee, which would devote itself to keeping Simon's bank account in a healthy state. This would remove such a burden from the full-time workers and would involve a variety of other people in Simon work. There was a growing realisation, which was to develop further in later years, that the organisation needed every kind of talent which was available to it. Sally Edwards, an experienced fund-raiser, was co-opted onto the fund-raising committee. The late Frank Maguire, a constant figure in Simon over the years, was also a member. As a result of the efforts of this committee the 1972 flag days were a great success.

Dick Shannon continued to work as administrator for Dublin Simon until May 1973. He received as payment the current full-time worker allowance of £3.50 a week and his keep. He was a key person at this stage, being able to give valuable advice to the workers on the quays as a result of his own experience. At the same time he provided a sense of continuity in Dublin Simon, which was of the utmost importance when dealing with the general public.

An important development during this era was the establishment of the Simon National Office in March 1972. Simon communities had been in existence in Limerick since 1969, and in Cork, Belfast and Waterford since 1971. The communities maintained contact with each other, albeit on an informal basis. Dublin Simon had, in fact, provided the Cork community with their first full-time worker in 1971. Dermot McMahon was anxious to create a national identity for the Simon Community and to facilitate better communications and co-operation between the individual communities.

In the early months of 1972, a number of meetings were held, where the possibility of having a central office, which would employ a National Co-ordinator, was tentatively explored. By March, it was agreed by all the communities involved that Dermot McMahon himself should fill this post. His salary and expenses were to be paid by grants from each of the communities according to their means and the situation was to be reviewed after one year. Although the original terms of reference for the national office were extremely wide, most of Dermot's initial efforts went into the recruitment of full-time workers.

Dublin Simon had given a good deal of thought to the recruitment and assessment of full-time workers. Committee members and former full-time workers had reflected on the qualities necessary in the prospective worker; issues such as time off, holidays and provision of a workers' flat had also come under considerable discussion. The other Irish communities were largely dependent on English workers or on people who just turned up at the door. When the national office was set up, it was decided to recruit workers on a national basis; afterwards they could be assigned to specific communities.

Dermot McMahon had been instrumental in working out a model for assessment interviews within Dublin Simon. Together with Ian Hart, another committee representative and at least one member of the full-time worker force, he had been conducting interviews successfully for over a year. For prospective workers such an interview had a dual function. It gave them the opportunity to express what it was that attracted them to Simon work, and to ask further questions about the nature of the work. It also meant that they would be challenged by the assessment committee to think a little more deeply about their motivation, attitudes to physical violence, and ability to cope under stress.

The interview often lasted for up to three quarters of an hour and left the prospective worker feeling exhausted. Nevertheless it usually gave the assessment team enough evidence on which to make a balanced judgement. Worker welfare is an issue which any voluntary organisation must be prepared to take seriously. An organisation like Simon, which was asking its full-time workers not only to work, but to live, in a very difficult situation, was showing a considerable degree of maturity in having a proper selection procedure.

Dermot's main concern, then, when he took up his post as National Co-ordinator, was to recruit workers on a national level, mainly through newspaper advertisements, and to ensure that all applicants underwent the same form of assessment. The model he used was similar to that which had been in use in Dublin Simon, and it was from the Dublin Committee and the former full-time worker force that he drew the other members of the national assessment committee. Thus there was a close link between the Dublin Community and the National Office, which exists to the present day.

After the interview, workers were assigned to particular communities. Their preferences were, of course, taken into consideration. Throughout 1972 there was great co-operation between the various communities. Situations arose where an experienced worker was needed on a particular project; through the National Co-ordinator it was possible to get volunteers to transfer from one community to another.

Although those involved may not have realised it at the time, this was the real beginning of the Simon Community as a national organisation. The links were being forged through friendship and support. Dermot visited all the communities regularly and became acquainted with the workers and the residents. Residents began to take an interest in what was happening outside their own community; occasionally arrangements were made for them to transfer from one city to another. National meetings, which were attended by delegates from each community, were held regularly. Simon Ireland was established and gaining stability. These close links between the communities continued. Dublin Simon contributed financially to the Belfast community when it was needy in the seventies. Dolores Whelan, who had strong links with Dublin Simon founded the Dundalk community in 1973. And in 1980, when Galway Simon was set up, the Dublin community contributed £2,000.

While the internal bonds between the various Simon communities strengthened, the National Co-ordinator was also concerned that media coverage would reflect this image of Simon as a national organisation with a definite policy and a mature approach towards its work with the homeless and rootless. Eugene McEldowney of the *Irish Times* wrote a number of articles about Simon during this period. One of them dealt with full-time Simon work, and gave a realistic impression of what was then involved. The following extract is an example of the kind of honest, sensitive press coverage which Dermot McMahon was seeking:

> If you thought that working for Simon meant getting a warm glow from handing out soup to grateful derelicts before skipping off to the next debutante's ball, forget it. You'll be lucky if you get beyond the first interview. Which is probably just as well. It means that you and Simon are both spared the embarrassment of the inevitable crack-up when you find out what it really is about.
>
> Simon is about caring. It's about living twenty-four hours a day with alcoholics and drug-abusers and ex-mental patients, under the same roof. It's about cadging vegetables from early morning traders so there'll be something to put in the stew you'll have to make when you get back to the wet house. It's about trying to put a roaring drunk to bed when he doesn't want to go. It's about getting jolted out of your sleep at about four o'clock in the morning when some other drunk decides he does want to go, but hasn't seen the necessity of getting back to the house before closing time. Sometimes it's about giving out soup . . . .
>
> If they [the assessment group] think you might work out they'll accept you into the Community on the understanding that you will work for a probationary period of one month. At the end of this time you will be assessed again and if you are still found to be suitable you will be accepted as a full-time Simon worker . . . .
>
> You will work a 120 hour week and be paid an allowance

of three pounds fifty pence a week with an additional one pound for the first week so you can insure your personal belongings. You will have a long week-end off every six weeks and nine days holidays every three months. During your holiday you will receive an allowance of £20 and when you finally decide to leave the Community you will receive a similar allowance. When you join Simon you will join a truly democratic Community. This means that all decisions are taken on a group basis after discussion and argument. It also means that when you join you leave some of your independence behind. Your work will involve cooking, cleaning, consoling. You will visit hospitals and prisons. You will speak in Court and also in schools and clubs. You will attend sensitivity groups where you will be encouraged to let off steam by complaining frankly about whatever happens to be bothering you.

Simon has three full-time communities in Ireland, Belfast, Dublin and Cork. Workers are needed for each. If you feel that you would be able to stick the life, for at least six months, they will be glad to hear from you. Minimum age is 19.

(*Irish Times*, 11 November 1972)

Dermot McMahon, as National Co-Ordinator, and Dick Shannon, as Administrator of Dublin Simon, worked closely with each other from mid-1972 until May 1973. Initially both offices were in 42 Harcourt Street; when the national office moved temporarily to a rented basement in D'Olier Street, Dick found himself dividing his time between the two offices. In May 1973 he left Dublin Simon and took up the post of Assistant National Co-Ordinator. When Dermot withdrew from full-time involvement with Simon, in order to study for a social science degree in Trinity College, Dick became National Co-Ordinator; he still holds that post, but his title now is National Director. Meanwhile another full-time worker, John Riordan, became Administrator with Dublin Simon. He, too, received a full-time worker allowance and his keep. He was the last Administrator to be paid in this fashion. In October 1973, the Dublin Simon Executive Committee agreed to 'employ' an administration team. Frank Sweeney, in his Chairman's report to the annual general meeting for 1973, explained the reasons for this decision:

> In an effort to meet the demands of a voluntary organisation of the seventies, Simon has most recently set up an administration team of two, backed by a full-time secretary. This is expected to lead to a more organised and co-ordinated effort from all, a better public image and greater concentration of fund-raising.

This decision marked the beginning of a new era for the Community.

Organisational development

Throughout the early seventies there were two forces at work in the shaping of Dublin Simon policy. On the one hand, there was the Executive Committee, the legal directors of the Community. Some members had been involved from the beginning. They provided a sense of continuity. Frank Sweeney and Bob Cashman retained their positions as Chairman and Vice Chairman, respectively, until June 1974. Ian Hart was continuously a member almost from the start until December 1975. On the other hand there were the workers, who organised themselves under full-time worker leaders.

Until autumn 1973 the two key positions among the full-time workers were those of Administrator and Community Leader. The workers who held these positions were ex officio Committee members, as were house leaders and a co-worker representative. The worker leaders reported directly to the Committee; they also saw themselves as policy makers in conjunction with the Committee. In fact the distinction between Committee members and full-time workers was not as clear as one might imagine. Several former full-time workers, such as Ray Smyth and Justin O'Brien, served on the Committee. Full-time workers of long standing and Committee members tended to socialise with each other. As a result there was reasonably good communication between the two groups, and policy was thrashed out with great intensity at Committee meetings.

One of the issues that was discussed interminably in the course of 1973 was the need for a more professional approach to administration. The Community was growing in size. A greater effort was needed in the area of planned, consistent fund-raising. Communication with the general public on homelessness and related issues needed attention. Such improvements could not, it was argued, be achieved through the efforts of a full-time worker team. It was unrealistic to expect men and women in their twenties to work indefinitely for the princely sum of £5.00 a week pocket money and their keep in a Simon house. For this reason and because of the intensity of the work, full-time workers, by definition, could only stick the work for a limited period. As a result, a high turnover was inevitable.

Gradually the Committee came to the conclusion that it was necessary to employ an administration team. Preference would be given to former full-time workers and co-workers, those who had a feeling for the Simon task. This, it was thought, would ensure that there would be a good relationship between full-time workers and office workers. So an administration team emerged from the very heart of the Community.

Frank O'Leary, the Franciscan priest, had been a soup-runner since 1970; he had also served as a Committee member. He now took up the post of Administrator, which involved looking after major house management problems and full-time worker problems, as well as being responsible for fund-raising. Felicity Casserly had been a full-time worker for a year, during five months of which she occupied the post of Community Leader. She was now appointed Deputy Administrator. Her work involved recruiting and co-ordinating the efforts of part-time workers, attending weekly full-time worker meetings, and ensuring that the Simon houses had sufficient supplies of foodstuffs, clothing and bedding. Noeleen Day, who had been a full-time worker in both Dublin and Cork, and who had also assisted Dermot McMahon on the administrative front when he was setting up the National Office, was now appointed to the post of secretary. Their salaries were in the region of £1,000 per annum.

In effect, the work required from these three staff members could not be pigeon-holed as neatly as their job descriptions might imply. Their areas overlapped a great deal. Often, if only one of the team was in the office, he or she dealt with urgent issues as they arose. This flexibility of approach was possible because each member of the staff already had an intimate knowledge of Simon affairs. Felicity Casserly told me that the dominant atmosphere during the early months of this regime was one of enthusiasm and co-operation within the Community. The administration team was regularly in touch with the Committee, and in constant touch with the Simon houses. Full-time workers felt supported by the office staff, knowing that their requirements would be dealt with promptly.

Public relations work now fell to the administration team. This removed a burden from the full-time workers and allowed them to devote their time and energy to the running of the houses and welfare of the residents. Co-workers also benefited. Felicity worked hard to co-ordinate their efforts and to make them feel part of the Community. *Link*, an internal newsletter which had been appearing spasmodically during 1973, was now put to good use in an effort to improve internal communication. Simon had grown, and it was no longer possible for full-time worker representatives from all the projects to be involved in every policy discussion; they had to trust those involved in administration to report their views.

A burning question at this time was whether or not Simon should continue to accept premises, on a caretaker's agreement, from individuals or companies who were involved in property speculation. This arose particularly in relation to the houses in Northumberland Square, located off Abbey Street in the city centre. In October 1972 Simon had moved a small group of residents who liked a peaceful life, into one vacant house in this square, which had been acquired by the Irish Life Assurance Company for development purposes. The following summer nine more houses, all of the two up, two down variety, became available.

There was considerable discussion as to whether these houses should be accepted. The Committee had been told that Simon could certainly have them for six months and, possibly, for up to two years. Some workers and Committee members were in favour because of the difficulties they were encountering on the quays, having a 'wet' house and 'dry' house situated side by side. But there was also opposition from within the worker force. Some were of the opinion that Simon residents who had lived in a community house should not now be split up into smaller units. Others, more political in their opposition, questioned the morality of Simon, an organisation which was founded to campaign on behalf of the homeless, being involved in deals with property speculators.

It was finally decided, at Committee level, to accept the nine houses in the square. Immediately they became available to Simon, Official Sinn Féin moved a family of ten, from Northern Ireland, into one of them as squatters. A meeting, which was subsequently held between representatives of Simon and of Sinn Féin, failed to resolve the issue. An indication of the strained relationship between the two organisations can be gleaned from a subsequent editorial in Sinn Féin's publication, *The United Irishman*, which was entitled 'Using Charity to Beat the Poor'. The editorial commented: 'On the night of Tuesday, July 24th, a family moved into Number 2, Northumberland Square. Consternation! Irish Life imitated the Cheshire Cat and stated that the problem was Simon's. Compliments were exchanged – even the old chestnut about being "non-political" and "using homeless families for political advantage" were hauled out by Simon representatives. Using a charitable organisation as a method of scaring off the homeless is, it seems, less reprehensible.' The squatters remained in Northumberland Square. Meanwhile five of the other houses were speedily prepared for occupation.

Residents from the 'dry' house were divided into smaller units among these houses. Another house, which contained an office, was also fitted with baths and showers. Two additional houses were used – one as a workshop and another as a recreation centre. The original house, which had become home for some of the quieter residents, continued as an independent unit. Some of the Simon workers hoped that this diverse group of people would settle down to a quiet, comfortable existence as a self-contained city centre community, but such hopes were soon dashed.

Life in Northumberland Square was fraught with great difficulty almost from the start. The 'no drink' rule which had operated in the 'dry' house posed a problem here. Among the residents there were two groups who enjoyed an occasional drink – eight elderly people and the four men who had been living in the Square for over a year. These residents occupied numbers 12, 13 and 14. Living in numbers 3, 4 and 5 were the residents who tended to have a genuine drink problem;

they saw no reason why they should be barred for drinking if their fellow-residents were not. In fact it was virtually impossible to bar anyone. The small houses were easily broken into, and residents who were drunk and angry tended to congregate on the pavement in the middle of the Square, disturbing the whole community. Early in 1974 there was a worker shortage; for the few full-time workers who were involved, the period was exhausting and frayed nerves and quick tempers were much in evidence.

Many of the residents were obviously unhappy. One couple, a common-law husband and wife, had enjoyed great status in Sarsfield Quay, they had been in charge of the kitchen. They now lived in a house on their own with one worker and felt isolated from the group. Another resident came home one night and broke all the windows. The style of the houses which were small and low and easily accessible, made such a disruptive occurrence possible. A sense of community had begun to grow among the group who had lived in Sarsfield Quay, but that had happened in the context of a controlled framework with everyone living under the same roof and sharing kitchen and living-room facilities. The more open environment in the Square made the possibility of such a controlled framework virtually impossible. The full-time workers, also, experienced a sense of isolation and frustration on account of this.

For the four men who had been living happily in number 12 before the influx, the whole situation was extremely disturbing. Their quiet home life was harshly disrupted. Simon members who witnessed this were among those who later fought hard to ensure that such residents would be given the chance to settle again, in a small house in a quiet residential area.

Internal conflict

The Executive Committee was aware of the difficult atmosphere that prevailed in the Square. The ex-worker members who had, in effect, decided on the project began to realise that some of the problems might have been foreseen. Around this time there was a growing awareness, due to mistakes having been made, that greater clarity was needed in relation to policy and planning within Simon.

An instance of internal conflict which arose in June 1974, in relation to vacating the houses in Northumberland Square, highlighted this need. Despite the misgivings that existed from time to time among Simon workers about involvement with property speculators, the Simon Committee had agreed to sign a caretaker's agreement with Irish Life in autumn 1973. Bob Cashman, alone, signed this agreement. He was acting as Chairman at the time, on account of Frank Sweeney's absence due to illness. By March 1974 the Simon administration had been told that they would have to vacate the houses in the near future. In June the final notice, of three weeks, was given. This amounted to a crisis situation in Simon as alternative accommodation had to be found.

At this stage, however, the whole question of the Simon Community as a campaigning body, and its relationship with property developers, flared up again. A group of full-time workers in the Square made it known forcefully that they did not approve of Simon honouring a caretaker's agreement with Irish Life. Their point of view is represented in a set of policy proposals, dating from this period:

> If a genuine attempt is made to restore the idealism of Simon then it should firstly have an impact on our dealings with property developers. We feel that it is completely contradictory for Simon to deal with people who are destroying houses and communities. We are only being used as security by such people and though it may benefit our residents we are contributing to one of the major problems of homelessness in the city. As far as possible any dealings with property developers should be avoided. Instead we should make more vigorous efforts to force the Corporation or Eastern Health Board to live up to their responsibilities. Simon is well-known and respected in Dublin and we are sure that the public would support us in our search for houses from these bodies.
>
> It is also necessary that Simon should reaffirm its commitment to being an alerting body which works for social changes. We should be prepared to speak for the people we work with and criticise the society that rejects them and the lack of provisions to help them. As an organisation which says that it cares for the homeless we should also be concerned with the wider problem of homelessness in the

> city and not confine ourselves merely to the people we deal with directly. We should help in highlighting the housing crisis in Dublin and do what we can to alleviate it . . . .
>
> . . . If Simon is not prepared to become more vocal and more radical there is a danger of it becoming yet another respectable charity who will accept the victims of an unjust society without criticising the society itself. We should be aware of how organisations such as Simon are used as society's dumping ground and how we are, to an extent, helping to support this type of society by dealing with its rejects.

The workers who held these views decided to challenge the Simon Committee on the issue; they threatened to squat in the houses in the square beyond the deadline of July 1st. These workers had the support of some co-workers in the Community.

When the Committee realised that the workers were serious about their intention to squat, they formally dismissed them. They were, however, left with the practical problem of getting them out of the Square. On this issue, the Committee itself was split. Frank Sweeney and Bob Cashman proposed that they seek an injunction to bar the rebel workers. The other Committee members opposed this, on the grounds that in so doing they would violate the Simon tradition of settling disputes without recourse to the law. Instead they were in favour of negotiating with the squatters. At this meeting, on July 19th, Frank Sweeney and Bob Cashman resigned. They did so for the following reasons:

> 1. A chairman and vice-chairman, who had lost the support of their committee, could not continue in office;
> 2. We were tired of doing the 'dirty' work of dealing with property developers and public authorities;
> 3. The time had come for the younger members to do these things, when they would learn that it was not as simple as it might seem;
> 4. We had other commitments which were being neglected because of the disproportionate time Simon was taking up.
>
> (From a letter written by Bob Cashman to Ian Hart)

In the negotiations which followed between the squatters and the now depleted Committee, a resolution was finally worked out. The workers left the Square on July 24th. At the same time Simon issued a public statement expressing sympathy for their cause. Simon acknowledged that the reason the workers were about to vacate the Square was because they did not want to force Simon to violate its own principles by seeking an injunction against them. Simon also agreed to support a family which had been squatting in the Square for some time in its search for new housing.

While this dispute was in progress the administration team, in conjunction with some Committee members, had been putting their energies into finding alternative accommodation for their residents. They succeeded in finding housing for all of them, but not without once again resorting to a caretaker's agreement in one instance. It was at this time, also, that they purchased their first house – in Melrose Avenue in Fairview.

While the Committee was going through the upheaval resulting from the loss of two of its older, experienced members, the administration team proved its worth. The residents were quietly moved to three different locations. Fund-raising activities continued. And the office was run in a professional manner.

Meanwhile Ray Smyth and Justin O'Brien, both former full-time workers, were elected temporarily as chairman and vice chairman of the Executive Committee. It was a difficult time for the Committee members. Their confidence had been shaken by the dispute. They felt keenly the loss of Frank Sweeney and Bob Cashman, both of whom had valuable contacts and experience. They were a younger Committee now, and they had to learn how to run the show alone.

In the months leading up to the 1974 annual general meeting they experienced difficulty reaching decisions. Every issue tended to be discussed from countless points of view. In September, a sub-committee was set up to formulate policy for the following year. This group, in their subsequent report, admitted that the real conflict within Simon was between the workers and the Committee. No policy would be properly implemented until there was complete agreement between these two bodies. This realisation highlighted the need for new structures to facilitate better communication and management.

In the autumn there were two changes in the administration team. Felicity Casserly and Noeleen Day left. Maureen Barry, who had been a co-worker for many years, took leave of absence from her Aer Lingus job, and filled the post of secretary. Paul Harrison, a quays co-worker with a background in advertising, became assistant administrator. Frank O'Leary continued in his job as Administrator and this provided a valuable continuity link.

The 1974 Annual General Meeting, held that October, was disrupted by some of the night shelter residents, who were protesting about conditions on Sarsfield Quay. The meeting was adjourned because the residents concerned were drunk; it was reconvened and a new Committee was elected. Ray Smyth and Justin O'Brien were re-elected as chairman and vice chairman.

By this stage, the policy sub-committee had come up with some new organisational proposals. A co-worker council was to be set up in order to allow various groups of such workers to establish adequate links with each other. This council would meet regularly and would have one representative on the Executive Committee. Management committees were to be set up for the night shelter and for each of the residential houses – now three in number. Each management committee would be chaired by a member of the Executive Committee. Other members would include a worker, a co-worker, a resident and, it was hoped, a neighbour from the area. The task of such a committee was to supervise the day-to-day management of the house, including the welfare of the residents and full-time workers. It would report back regularly to the Executive Committee, and any major decision would have to be taken at that level.

By January 1975 the co-worker council had begun to meet regularly. By February the house management committees had been set up. This meant that issues which until then had been discussed at Executive Committee level, could now be dealt with by the individual management committees. As a result the Executive meetings were not so exhausting or frustrating.

Another decision was also taken at this stage – to employ

a qualified social worker. This decision was not implemented until July 1975. The social worker who was appointed to the post, at a social worker's salary, was none other than John Long, who had been a full-time worker in Winetavern Street. So the tendency to employ staff who already understood the nature and aims of the Community was continued. By the middle of 1975, Dublin Simon had quite a sophisticated organisational structure. The respective tasks of full-time workers, administrative staff and Committee members had been agreed upon, and a serious attempt was being made to clarify Simon policy.

Wanted – good as new clothes . . .

As Simon developed over the years, it began to need more and more money. Initially the organisation had few overheads. As it began to expand, fund-raising became a major issue. Donations were a godsend. Flag-days and carol-singing restored the bank account to health in the winter months. But Simon badly needed some kind of regular income. The idea of the Simon shop stemmed from this need.

One summer afternoon in 1984, having bought my fruit and vegetables from the witty, weather-beaten traders at the top of Camden Street, I crossed the road to pay a visit to this establishment. Situated on a corner, it has a black, tiled frontage and two big, bright windows with attractive hanging plants. Just one word – SIMON – in large, white capitals lets prospective customers know whom they are supporting. Dublin Simon has this premises on lease and paid an annual rent of £8,500 in 1983.

The shop, as it is known among Community members, was not always so well housed. It started as a second-hand clothes shop in January 1973 in a dark, draughty ill-equipped premises opposite the Academy cinema in Pearse Street. Those working there at the beginning had little experience in such ventures and stood dumbfounded as dealers came in and began to bargain for 'lots' of their precious stock. They learned quickly, and they realised the need for premises in a more central location. Between that time and June 1977, Simon managed to get rent-free premises, on caretaker agreements, in a variety of locations – Stephen's Green, Harcourt Street, Lower Baggot Street. The 1975 Annual Report recognised the shop as making 'a major contribution to funds', when the accounts showed its income to be £11,500.

By the end of 1977, when it became apparent that the shop would have to move yet again, the Executive Committee decided, after much discussion, to rent the present premises in Camden Street. It was a wise move. The public now know where Simon is, and it has worked financially too. In 1986 Dublin Simon bought this premises.

On the afternoon of my visit, Kathleen Cahalane and Phyllis Lynch were on duty. They are both Simon 'oldies' and have been involved in the shop since the start. Kathleen is a small, spry middle-aged woman, who has reared her family – Denis, her son, has figured earlier in the Simon story. She shares responsibility for the management of the shop with Marie Trundle. Together they liaise with Frank Maguire, a member of the Executive Committee. Either Kathleen or Marie is always on the premises during business hours – Tuesday to Friday, 11 am to 5 pm, Saturday, 11 am to 2 pm. There are about twenty other women involved in the venture; some do a morning or afternoon each week, others work a full day. They still need volunteers who will commit themselves definitely to at least one period a week.

Phyllis Lynch is a widow, with three teen-age children. She did a Simon soup-run for two years in the early seventies and also collected the Health Board supplies of disinfectant, detergent, toilet-paper etc. from James Street and delivered them to the houses on the quays. I distinctly remember, during my own stint as a full-time worker, how welcome she was with her precious supplies. Disinfectant and toilet-paper were real luxuries; if we ran out before the end of the month our meagre budget rarely allowed us to purchase replacements. Phyllis now works in the shop for three periods a week and she knows most of the regular customers. Local people use the shop, of course, but customers also come, she told me, from Terenure and Rathfarnham, Crumlin and Ringsend. Some people drop in every day to see if there are any new bargains.

The shop now stocks 'good' second-hand clothes, books, household items, and bric-a-brac. On the book shelf, among a collection of old hardbacks, I found paperback editions of novels by D.H. Lawrence and Taylor Caldwell, as well as a book by H.J. Eysenck entitled *You and Neurosis*. I was tempted to have a quick flick through the latter in search of self-knowledge, but I restrained myself. Old school books and magazines were also on sale. On another shelf there was a wide variety of items – a globe, rolls of wallpaper, toys in good condition and some crockery. Underneath were a couple of suitcases. Both ladies' and gents' shoes were selling for 50p a pair. Phyllis explained that they had to keep a sharp eye on that section of the shop – some customers were known to arrive wearing one pair of shoes and leave wearing another without any commercial transaction taking place. On one occasion the evidence of such an occurrence took the form of a most unpleasant odour.

In the window which faced onto Camden Street stood a full-size model dummy tastefully decked out in a check suit and navy polo-neck. She was accompanied by two half-sized dummies on stands – each showing a jacket off to advantage. Inside there was a small area cordoned off by a counter, on which stood a rather battered cash register. Alongside the front window stood a rail of gents' suits, jackets and coats. Most of them were in excellent condition. A tweed sports jacket was priced at £3.50. As I looked through the garments on the rack, a young man came in looking for a suit. Kathleen explained that there was no fitting room; he could try on the jacket and she would measure the width and length of the trousers, if he knew his measurements. He did, and after five minutes' negotiation he was the proud possessor of a smart, charcoal grey suit, which had only cost him £8.00. He hummed to himself as he left the shop. In the meantime I had wandered over towards the women's clothes rack. There was a great selection of blouses, skirts and jeans – all in good condition and reasonably priced. A black velvet jacket was priced at £3.50, while the Indian padded variety was selling for £2.00.

Kathleen explained that they are now only interested in clothes that are still in fashion, clean and in good condition. She and Marie do most of the sorting in a room at the back of the shop. Much of what is given to them is too old or tatty to sell to the public. They either give it to the Simon work project or sell it in lots to the local dealers. After years of experience in the business Kathleen reckons she knows what will sell. There is no point having the shop cluttered with rubbish; this does not entice customers. She told me that they had quite recently spent some money in an effort to improve the shop. New clothes racks and dump baskets were bought. The place was freshly painted, and lights were installed in the windows with dark, wintry afternoons in mind. All this has helped business.

I wondered if Simon residents ever visited the shop. Apparently they do occasionally, to pass the time of day or beg the fare home or complain about lack of clothes supplies in the shelter. The women also see the shop as a public relations effort for Dublin Simon. They have literature available about the Community and are able to advise people who enquire about the various forms of co-worker activities. The staff in Camden Street see themselves as very much part of Dublin Simon. They are familiar with the philosophy of the Community and are in sympathy with its objectives. The work they do as volunteers is their contribution towards rectifying the plight of the homeless in Dublin.

5

WHO IS BEING UNFAIR?

Prejudice – an emotional short-cut?

Would it surprise you to discover that you are a trifle intolerant at times? That you make judgements about individuals and groups without adequate evidence? That the sometimes misguided attitudes with which you grew up still influence many of your reactions? That, on occasion, you make up your mind rather hastily and are not flexible enough to change it even in the face of convincing evidence? In short, would it shock you to discover that you are quite a prejudiced human being?

Prejudice, the sociologists tell us, is a negative attitude towards an individual, because that individual is a member of a stigmatised group. Such an attitude can give rise to stereotyped statements – 'the Irish are a lazy race' or 'women are bad drivers'. Thus, the individual is not judged objectively on his or her own merits, but is immediately branded. In 1973, Dr Mícheál MacGréil directed a research team which carried out a survey of social attitudes towards minority groups among a random sample of three thousand adults living in the greater Dublin area. On the positive side, he discovered a high degree of tolerance towards widows, unmarried mothers and deserted wives. But the results of the survey also pointed to a relatively high degree of latent racialism, and such minority groups as itinerants, communists, the unemployed, alcoholics, drug-addicts, criminals and atheists were regarded with a high degree of intolerance (*Prejudice and Tolerance in Ireland*, Research Section, College of Industrial Relations, 1977). In 1979, when Dr MacGréil was invited to address the National Conference of the Irish Simon communities, he pointed out that the Simon-type client did not constitute one specific stimulus category in his research, but he gave his own view on how the Irish public regarded the homeless person:

> The problem with the 'down and outs' who seek help from Simon is that they probably carry the stigma of 'unemployed', 'heavy drinker', 'alcoholic', 'drug addict', and in some people's minds, that of 'criminal'.
>
> Such a combination of negative categories is likely to reinforce severe prejudices against the dosser. The attitudes of people against the above listed social stimulus categories have been singularly severe.
>
> If my hypothesis is true, the dosser is a composite social category of four or five of the most disliked categories in our society.
>
> (From Dr MacGréil's Address)

If we accept Mícheál MacGréil's hypothesis, we are in fact accepting that many people in Irish society have learned, possibly as children, to dislike and distrust homeless people. How does this happen? Why do some people retain social attitudes learned in childhood, while others are flexible enough to change when faced with contrary evidence? To what extent do the media reinforce negative attitudes towards such minority groups, by presenting their members as stereotypes rather than as unique individuals each with his or her own story? Perhaps most important of all, what effect do these negative attitudes have on homeless people, if they experience them repeatedly over a number of years? These are important questions, and I believe that they need to be explored if we wish, as a society, to become more just, more tolerant, and ultimately more loving.

Drawing on sociological research once more, we learn that an attitude has three components. Firstly we *believe* something to be true about, for example, all black men; as a result we have certain *feelings* towards all black men; eventually, if we are in a situation where *action* is called for, we will act as a result of those beliefs and feelings: we might, for example, on the basis of a negative attitude towards black males, decide to vote against them having certain civil rights. The fact that we may never have spoken to an individual black man in our lives, may never have heard his story or discovered anything about his culture, does not impinge on us. We see all black men as belonging to a group which we perceive to have negative qualities and as a result we dislike and may decide to persecute all members of this group. This kind of attitude can be passed down from generation to generation through the socialisation process; at home children learn attitudes from their parents, in school they come to accept the dominant societal values. So it can happen, Mícheál MacGréil argues, that a majority within a society can come to hold a particular negative attitude. At this point it has already become part of the culture which Mícheál MacGréil defines as 'the convictions people have, the values they have, and the norms of behaviour they have accepted as proper for human society'. Such a negative attitude is also regularly reinforced, albeit unwittingly, by the media. If an Irish woman is raped by an African student, this story is likely to receive wide media coverage; if she is raped by an Irish man of high standing, it is quite possible that the facts will be distorted and the case quashed. Thus a negative attitude which is already culturally acceptable is further reinforced.

What is frightening about this analysis of how negative social attitudes develop and are transmitted is that the evidence on which such deeply held convictions are based is usually inadequate, selective or obsolete. So we are, in fact, stigmatising individuals who belong to minority groups, without giving them even a ghost of a chance to prove that they do not have *all* the negative characteristics that we presume them to have. They, in turn, cannot remain unaffected by such a hostile attitude from the majority group in their society, so we must take into account what is known sociologically as the 'vicious circle theory'. Dr MacGréil describes this theory in relation to the homeless.

> For example, if social attitudes towards vagrants are negative, the vagrants will be treated badly by society and their poverty and deprivation will become worse. This will force them to a greater desire for alcohol and tempt them to procure money by means of theft and deception, thus making them appear even more degraded in public. As a result, the initial negative social attitudes will be reinforced and the behaviour becomes more negative resulting in frequent arrest, summary trials and regular insulation in prison . . . .

> The people you meet in Simon have gone the full run of the vicious circle theory on its downward track; they were defined negatively and they became what they were defined. If you define a situation as real, it becomes real as a consequence of the definition, because public definition is a very powerful conditioner of people. Further, the people who are themselves ill-defined eventually accept the public definition themselves. This is a very sad situation.
>
> (From Mícheál MacGréil's Address)

If we accept that, as a society, we are quite prejudiced against certain minority groups, who suffer greatly as a result, and if we accept that at least some of the social attitudes of our culture are based on faulty or selective evidence, what can we do about changing these attitudes? Again, in relation to the homeless, Mícheál MacGréil makes the following comment:

> To change public opinion in their (the dossers') favour, we would have to try and educate the people to have a more sympathetic understanding . . . or try to get them to desist from categorising individuals into negative stereotypes. In this connection the role of fear, insecurity and anxiety in producing a psychological condition conducive to prejudice must be noted. People need to be reassured and the best way to do this is through favourable and positive contact.

Favourable and positive contact – that is, meeting and relating to *individuals* who belong to minority groups, and allowing ourselves to be surprised and delighted by the outcome – *is* probably the most powerful way of working towards a fairer outlook. But this kind of contact requires courage. It is easier to mix simply with 'our own', those who dress like us, speak like us, and think like us. There is a risk involved in breaking out of our comfortable social groups; to do so in order to make contact with the travellers or with other homeless people may seem like sheer folly to many. To donate old furniture or used clothes or even sums of money to help these people is one thing; actually to meet them, chat with them, perhaps allow ourselves to like them is something else entirely. We may be frightened by the behaviour of some of the homeless, or indeed we may have some of our property stolen, but perhaps the biggest risk that we will run, by getting to know Sarah or Tommy as the individuals they are, is that we may be forced to re-examine our values or to change our attitudes. And changing our attitudes is a painful process, as it means going against the conditioning of a lifetime. In Matthew's gospel we are told a story which illustrates something of the intensity of this struggle for attitudinal change:

> Jesus left that place and withdrew to the region of Tyre and Sidon. Then out came a Canaanite woman from that district and started shouting, 'Sir, Son of David, take pity on me. My daughter is tormented by a devil.' But he answered her not a word. And his disciples went and pleaded with him. 'Give her what she wants,' they said, 'because she is shouting after us.' But he said in reply, 'I was sent only to the lost sheep of the House of Israel.' But the woman had come up and was kneeling at his feet. 'Lord,' she said, 'help me.' He replied, 'It is not fair to take the children's food and throw it to the house-dogs.' She retorted, 'Ah yes, Sir; but even house-dogs can eat the scraps that fall from their master's table.' Then Jesus answered her, 'Woman, you have great faith. Let your wish be granted.' And from that moment her daughter was well again. (Mt 15: 21-28)

Jesus was a Jew, and had therefore grown up within a religious and cultural tradition which saw the Jews, and only the Jews, as the chosen people of God. In this story a Canaanite woman approaches him seeking help for her daughter, who was probably mentally ill. He ignores her, initially, as any good Jew would have done. Firstly she was a Canaanite, a member of a despised race. Secondly she was a woman and was pleading for her daughter; within the Jewish patriarchal system such a request might not have seemed important. Even when the disciples pleaded with him, Jesus was not prepared to help. The woman was not one of 'the lost sheep of the House of Israel'. Therefore he likened her to an animal scrounging for food. But she did not give up. And something about her, an individual who dared to speak for herself and demand justice, made Jesus change his mind and respond to her. He did so, not out of pity, but out of profound respect for the quality of her faith. Jesus conquered the prejudices of his upbringing because he allowed himself to encounter an individual Canaanite woman, and, against all the odds, to be transformed by her.

Apartheid – Irish style

The November 1976 edition of the *Simon Ireland Newsletter* carried an editorial by Dick Shannon in which he made the following statement:

> Events over the past month or two have added to the credibility and accuracy of Father MacGréil's findings. We have witnessed:
> 1) The decision by Simon to withdraw from Chapelizod because of opposition from local people.
> 2) The decision by the Samaritans to abandon plans for setting up a centre in a Dublin suburb because of opposition from local people.
> 3) The decision by Galway Corporation to deny travelling people homes in the Castlegar area because of opposition from local people.
>
> As more and more local communities decide to set up no-go areas and exclude deprived people from their midst, it must be obvious – even to the most casual observer – that prejudice and intolerance are now rampant in Irish society. A lot of the opposition and intolerance can be attributed to ignorance arising from the failure of the organisations involved to educate the general public.

So we discover that despite the warm support received by Simon from the Irish public in the early seventies, they, too, had by November 1976 encountered their own share of social prejudice. This prejudice came to a head when Dublin Simon attempted to integrate socially certain residents by setting up smaller home-like units in two residential areas.

Housing policy became a central issue for the Executive Committee of Dublin Simon in the middle of 1974. Until then they had simply been grateful to receive premises – whether on lease from the Corporation as in the case of 9 and 10 Sarsfield Quay, or on a caretaker's agreement from property developers, as in the case of 42 Harcourt Street and the houses in Northumberland Square. When, however, the conflict about vacating the latter premises arose, the validity of continuing to settle for temporary housing was called into question. Simon's priority was to provide 'home' for its residents, some of whom had come to rely on the Community for long-term care. Security and a sense of belonging were important to these men and women; their lives had already been marked by the fact that they did not have that most treasured possession – a fixed abode. And now, in Simon, that pattern was beginning to repeat itself. Some residents had lived in three different houses in the 1970-74 period; they had moved on, not always by their own choice, but rather as a result of developments in Simon policy. Moreover, as the Community grew in experience, long-term members came to realise that there were different categories of Simon residents. Some people were happy to stay on the quays, near their old haunts and within a stone's throw of the city centre. But there were others who needed a different environment. Some were trying to kick a drinking habit; they did not wish to meet their mates as soon as they stepped outside the door. And there were residents who were happy to run a small house with only minimal worker involvement as had been witnessed when the original group of four men moved to Northumberland Square. Clearly some kind of tier system was needed, if Simon were not to become institutional and inflexible in its approach. If such a tier system were to work, the question of the location of future Simon houses had to be seriously considered.

Shortly after the 1973 Annual General Meeting a sub-committee was set up to consider housing needs. The members of this committee realised that the time had come for Dublin Simon to begin purchasing its own houses. Only then could the Community choose suitable locations and provide stable, homely accommodation for long-term residents. Action was needed on the housing front, but committees tend to work slowly. When, in June 1974, Simon was asked to vacate the Irish Life Assurance Company property in Northumberland Square with only three weeks' notice, the Community had a crisis on its hands.

A few of the residents decided to fend for themselves, but accommodation had to be found immediately for twenty-two people who had quite varied needs. A house was bought in great haste, a cosy, terraced house on a quiet avenue in Fairview. Within weeks, seven Simon residents were living there. Local people did not know who had purchased the house until they saw their new neighbours being installed. They were extremely angry at not having been consulted by the Simon Community; and they refused to accept the excuse that Dublin Simon had been forced to act speedily. So 36 Melrose Avenue got off to a bad start. Unfortunately the pattern of relationship between Simon and the local residents did not improve with time. This house, however, did constitute 'home' for between five and eight of the more stable Simon residents over a period of seven years. These men and women were anxious to live normal, peaceful lives; they helped to run the house and care for each other – as members of a family might do. They took pride in entertaining their visitors. Like any family, they had their rows and their bad times also. But eventually they had to leave. They learned once again that they were unacceptable because they were perceived to be different and, therefore, potentially dangerous.

Meanwhile other Simon residents had moved yet again into temporary accommodation. A sizable house at 100 Lower Dorset Street was given to Simon on a caretaker's agreement by a property developer. It was a godsend as otherwise ten men and women, many of them older, chronic alcoholics, would have found themselves homeless once more. These residents wished to be near the city centre. Simon never had any intention of trying to integrate them into a suburban, residential area. But they, too, were forced to move on again fairly quickly. In the spring of 1975, Dublin Corporation wished to buy this house from the property developer. The Corporation insisted on vacant possession. The Simon Community pleaded for a caretaker's agreement for another year, as they were still faced with huge difficulties in finding suitable accommodation at a price they could afford. But the Corporation refused, although it did not actually begin to demolish the house until 1978. Meanwhile Simon managed to purchase 36 Seán MacDermott Street. This was an ideal location for the residents concerned who needed extra attention and a little bit of real comfort. This house is still 'home' for the senior citizens of the Simon Community.

The other small group of Simon residents moved from Northumberland Square into a flat at the top of 42 Harcourt Street. Each of these residents (four male, one female) had a history of psychiatric hospital care. They tended to be withdrawn and did not form relationships easily. Workers who knew them well suggested that they needed long-term, stable, residential care, in an atmosphere flexible enough to allow for their individuality and eccentricities. Heavy drinking was not a problem among this group; nor was violent behaviour, although strongly colourful language could be a feature of their gatherings. After about a year together in Harcourt Street, four out of the five were getting on well with each other, and taking varying degrees of responsibility in relation to the running of the household affairs. They had undoubtedly benefited by the move away from the Square, where there had been a good deal of noise and violence; an atmosphere of calm and a firm, but gentle, approach by the workers had done much to stabilise this little community of fragile individuals. But by September 1975 there were rumours abroad that the Harcourt Street house was to be sold. Once again the Simon Executive Committee had to make some decision about the future of a group of residents. There were differing points of view on this issue. One suggestion was that yet another temporary house should be found. Another possibility was to split these residents up and try to place them in other Simon projects, in Fairview, for example, or in welfare homes. But the Harcourt Street Management Committee had strong views on the issue:

> At the last Committee meeting when the futures of the Harcourt Street residents were discussed, it was decided that a temporary house would be the next step for them, and a final decision on buying a permanent house would be put off until other possibilities were exhausted.
>
> At that time the Harcourt Street Management Committee accepted the Executive Committee decision. However on reconsidering, and after discussions with Harcourt Street co-workers, we now agree that the decision was not satisfactory.
>
> We strongly feel that another temporary house would only continue the insecurity the residents have suffered up to now.

We ask for a more positive approach in the housing of these residents, instead of the present attitude which appears to be that only when all else fails will a permanent house be considered for them.

Leaving aside the problems we know exist in purchasing a house for Simon residents and concentrating on the welfare of the residents, we feel the encouraging fact that the Harcourt Street residents have adapted to each other during the past year points to a decision to continue efforts to stabilise this community.

Chapelizod residents say 'No'.

In fact, the Executive Committee really *had* tried to house the Harcourt Street residents. As early as October 1974 they had intended buying a corner house on Willow Park Avenue in Ballymun but they withdrew from the deal on account of opposition from local residents. Now, as a result of the convictions of those involved in the Harcourt Street project, they went househunting once more. By December 1975 they had found a suitable premises – a detached house with surrounding garden, in Chapelizod. Ian Hart, an Executive Member at that time, describes what happened next:

The Committee decided in December 1975 to buy a house in Chapelizod to replace the house in Harcourt Street as they had been asked to leave that house by its owner. People living in Chapelizod heard about this decision through 'Link' (the internal newsletter of Dublin Simon) and held a meeting in a local school the following month to announce their opposition to the plan. They were encouraged in this stance by members of the Fairview Residents' Association. Members of the Simon Committee, who had been invited to the meeting, tried to explain that the house would not be a night shelter but their attempts to reassure the people were fruitless. About this time local residents placed a picket on the shop of a brother of the owner of the house but were forced to withdraw the picket when an injunction was brought against them.

At the end of January the Committee reaffirmed the decision to buy the house and one-quarter of the money was paid as deposit. It emphasised in a letter to the Residents' Association (after the contract had been signed) that the house would be for six of their quietest residents and offered the Association a say in the management of the house. The house stood in its own grounds, unlike the Fairview house, and was some distance back from the road. A lane which passed by it was used by children going to school and this increased people's fear that Simon's clients would molest, or be a bad example to their children.

In early February a spokesman for the Residents' Association wrote to accuse Simon of reneging on an 'assurance' to the TD present at the January meeting that they would await the outcome of his motion to the Health Board before they purchased the house. The Committee sent letters to TDs, local councillors, and the Press about their plans for the house at this stage. They also invited the spokesman for the Chapelizod Residents to visit the Harcourt Street house to meet the people that Simon proposed to move to Chapelizod.

This letter was not acknowledged.

(*Dublin Simon Community 1971-1976: An Exploration*, ESRI, 1978, pp 123-4)

The following eight months proved to be exhausting and disturbing for the Simon Executive Committee. They decided in February to take possession of the house, but not to move any residents until further discussions had taken place. The Residents' Association would not agree to this. In the middle of March the Eastern Health Board intervened; they offered Simon a house on the North Circular Road in exchange for the one in Chapelizod. As a result of a subsequent meeting between Simon and representatives of the Residents' Association, chaired by a TD from the Chapelizod area, Simon decided to accept the house on the North Circular Road. At the beginning of April, however, the Eastern Health Board withdrew the offer of the house. Instead, they were prepared to make six places available in Health Board group homes. This was not acceptable to the Simon Committee. They resolved finally to close the deal, and to take possession of the Chapelizod house. The events that followered were unpleasant in the extreme:

At 4 o'clock on the afternoon of April 5, Monday, four

members of the Committee and Administration went to the house to take possession. A siren which had been rigged up by the neighbours went off bringing many angry people to the scene. Two members of the Simon group scaled a wall and gained entry while the other two were stopped by an angry crowd. The latter two members went to the local Garda station and returned to the house with an inspector and eight Gardaí. The combined party was still prevented from gaining access and, after a few minutes, the two Simon representatives asked the Gardaí not to use further force as this would permanently embitter the local community. The local residents believed that Simon had tried to gain possession of the house without notifying them of their intention. Some said they would allow the two Simon people still outside the house to visit the house under their escort. This offer was refused after consultation over the telephone with other Committee members at the office and, instead, a temporary injunction was obtained to stop the blockade, pickets and the use of the siren. The injunction was served on the crowd at 11.30 pm but they still refused entry and Simon were not prepared to ask the Gardaí to use force to obtain an entry. Nor would the Gardaí deliver food to the two members of the group inside the blockaded house, and, after the telephone had been cut, the two abandoned it the next day.

(*op. cit.*, pp 125-6)

The Simon Committee had not, in fact, tried to take possession of the house without notifying the people of Chapelizod. Letters had been posted from the GPO at 5 pm on Sunday, 4th April to the Residents' Association, TDs, and local councillors, informing them of Simon's intention. At a Committee meeting, which took place after the unpleasant confrontation, it was decided to write again to the Residents' Association to apologise for not having given more notice of the decision to take possession; to insist on Simon's right to occupy its house; to ask for a list of their objections to Simon using the house; and to inform them that Simon was prepared to enforce the injunction as a last resort.

Although a full injunction had been granted to Simon by the end of April, they did not use it to take possession, because they were requested by the Attorney General to await the outcome of an impending meeting of the Eastern Health Board. While the Eastern Health Board, Dublin Corporation, and the Department of Health were all, reputedly, seeking some solution to the problem, valuable time was being lost from Dublin Simon's standpoint. A further complication arose when ACRA (the Association of Combined Residents' Associations) offered to mediate between Simon and the Chapelizod Residents' Association. Simon agreed not to take possession while negotiations were in progress. The Chapelizod Residents' Association, however, proved unwilling to accept ACRA's mediation.

In mid-June the Simon Committee made a new proposal:

> Simon's Committee have proposed a legal covenant which would bind Simon to its word, and make it possible for the house to be closed down should that word be broken. After all, if Simon are to be honest in this matter we should not fear having an agreement sealed by a solicitor. Basically the covenant proposes that a house for homeless people be set up under the management of Dublin Simon. A committee would then be set up, comprising of two members of Simon, two from Chapelizod and two others. This committee would act as a watch dog over the house. Should it happen that a nuisance is being caused, the committee has the power to insist that the nuisance be stopped. If it is not, the committee would have the power to close the house down.
>
> (*Link*, July, 1976)

A draft of the covenant was sent to the Residents' Association as a discussion document. While Simon was awaiting a reply, the Harcourt Street house had to be vacated and the little group of residents were whisked away to the sea for a holiday in the hope that the situation would be resolved quickly. At a meeting held in July between Simon and the Residents' Association, the topic of the proposed covenant was avoided; the Chapelizod Residents were interested in the possibility of the Eastern Health Board running the house. By the time Simon had managed to clarify this issue with the Health Board, yet another month had passed. It transpired that while the Health Board would provide back-up services, they were not prepared, nor had they the money, to manage the house. By the end of September the Simon Committee had lost heart; they announced that they would not be moving into Chapelizod.

In the following months, the Chapelizod house was vandalised three times. It had to be restored before it could be put up for sale. Meanwhile two of the five Harcourt Street residents had been placed in other Simon houses; the other three were either in non-Simon hostels or sleeping rough. In the 1976 Annual General Report of the Dublin Simon Community, Justin O'Brien, Chairman of the Executive Committee, commented on the situation:

> The Committee undertook to rehouse some of the Harcourt Street residents and we bought a house in Chapelizod for them. We were opposed by the local community who resorted to varying tactics to stop us. Our position was always to establish a home with the consent of the local community. In this we were unsuccessful.
>
> We were unable to abate the fears and prejudices of the local people despite our many reasonable attempts. The issue became a notional issue and our organisation was subjected to criticism by the local politicians and the Residents' Association. The outcome of that issue will undoubtedly affect any plans we may have at a future date for housing some of our people in suburban areas.

A loophole in the law

While members of Dublin Simon were struggling to take possession of the house in Chapelizod, one of the forces working steadily against them was the Fairview and District Residents' Association. Simon, it has been noted, purchased a house in Melrose Avenue in July 1974. They did so in great haste and without informing local residents. This was undoubtedly a mistake. Those who suffered most as a result were the Simon residents who were exposed to precisely the kind of hostility and rejection from which they were hoping to escape. By this time Simon had clarified for themselves the difference between shelter work and the running of residential houses. Unfortunately the general public were not at all clear about this crucial distinction. The word 'Simon' conjured up particular images in the minds of many people – images which were threatening and terrifying, and Dublin Simon by mid-1974 had done little to change this situation. Much later, when considering the kind of problems being faced by the Simon Community in Limerick, Dick Shannon was still grappling with this issue:

> Why, we may ask, do we pose such a threat to local communities and councils? No doubt, sociologists in the future will have something to offer on why we have been rejected in Waterford, Ballymun, Chapelizod and now Limerick. Whatever the reasons, a factor worthy of consideration is the part which Simon, with the aid of the media, unwittingly played in presenting a distorted image of homeless people – particularly in earlier days. They were portrayed in emotive terms as winos, dossers, and as aggressive, violent and anti-social people. It is no wonder then that Residents' Associations should react so vehemently, and that some unscrupulous politicians, who do not give a damn about homeless people should exploit these fears.
>
> (*Simon Ireland Newsletter*, April, 1977)

If the Simon Community itself talks about 'Simon-type people' or 'our Simon people', it can hardly blame the general public, many of whom have never even spoken to a homeless person, for imagining that those who use the Simon service are a breed apart. But this is not the case. Simon is used by a variety of individuals, each with his or her own story. There are certain similarities between many of the stories, but this is true of any group of people – those who live in a particular village, those who choose to do volunteer service abroad, those who become members of religious orders. Yet we do not think of any of these groups as a breed apart. Moreover, within Simon different residents have different needs. Those who use the Shelter sometimes have a heavy drinking pattern; as a result they need shelter and food when they are drunk and possibly a degree of challenge when they are sober. There is nothing unusual about this. Any family in this country, who has a relative suffering from alcoholism, will be all too familiar with this pattern of need. One alcoholic goes home to his or her family, another goes 'home' to the Simon Shelter.

But as Dublin Simon developed it became evident that some residents who had originally just dropped in to the houses on Sarsfield Quay, as they might to any city hostel, eventually began to look on Simon as offering the possibility of 'home' in the long-term sense. Such men and women needed a lifestyle centred around the kind of normal, everyday routine to which most of us are accustomed. For some reason they had ended up in the city hostels and seemed to find it impossible to set up a home for themselves again. The house in Melrose Avenue was an attempt by Simon to provide such a home, with minimum worker support, for a small group of people.

Initially, due to the haste involved in the vacation of Northumberland Square, a couple of residents were moved into 36 Melrose Avenue who subsequently proved unable to cope in such an environment. But there were four men who lived in that house for seven years, in the company of one or two full-time workers, for whom life took on a new dimension. Despite the hostility of many of the local people, these men lived a simple, routine life which fulfilled many of their human needs. They had each other for company; they slept in small, cosy bedrooms; they were involved in the cooking and in the cleaning; birthdays were celebrated; those who enjoyed a social drink could have it now and again; former full-time workers who came back to visit, some of them from abroad, were welcomed and entertained. In short, these men began to experience again what most of us take for granted – ordinary human affection and a sense of belonging.

Mick was one of the men who lived in Melrose Avenue until 1981. I had been friendly with him during my period as a full-time worker on Sarsfield Quay. A tall, well-built man, his manner appears brusque at first. On further acquaintance, one discovers his dry wit and quiet good humour. He has an extraordinary memory; he can tell each former worker when they started to work in Simon, the day of the week, the date, and the year. When I met him recently he told me something of his own story.

He was of country stock, having grown up on a small farm in the midlands. As a young man he had worked footing turf, while living in a Bord na Móna hostel, which he enjoyed. When the turf station closed down in the fifties he went to

England where he stayed for eleven years, working on the buildings and in a factory. He came back to Dublin in the late sixties – a move he has been regretting ever since – and could not get work. Having lived in a couple of the city hostels for a while, he tried Simon in the early seventies.

'I don't know why I decided to stay,' he told me, 'and not go back to any of the other hostels. I had given up looking for work at that stage. The workers in Simon were different from the workers in the other hostels. Simon was more of a home, sure a hostel can't be a home, can it? I didn't know what to make of Ian Hart and the group meetings. I didn't talk at them very much. I didn't know very much about psychology.'

Mick moved from the Quays to a house in Northumberland Square in 1972. He liked living in a small house – with three other men and one worker. He did a bit of the cooking himself and got on well with the others. He moved to Melrose Avenue in July 1974 and lived there until May 1981.

'I was in Fairview about five weeks short of seven years,' he told me. 'I was happy living there. It was a terraced house with seven rooms and a bathroom. I shared a room with Jack. Simon had got better and better from the Quays to the Square to Fairview. But it was different coming to Seán MacDermott Street. The house was in an awful state. Now, though, I don't mind being back in the city centre.'

Mick is good company. An avid newspaper reader, he takes a great interest in current affairs. While he relies on the other Simon residents for his long-term friendships, the workers are an important part of his life; because of the steady turnover, he is constantly meeting new people, making new relationships. He enjoys discussing politics and has a lively interest in both national and international affairs. But his attitude to the law is cynical; experience has taught him not to expect too much from it. When I asked him if he was angry about having to leave the house in Melrose Avenue, he said:

'No, I don't feel angry towards the people in Fairview. There must be something wrong with them though, because no-one was doing them any harm. But they found some loophole in the law, didn't they? And the law's the law.'

A change of use

The Fairview and District Residents' Association did indeed find a loophole in the law. By February 1975 they were suggesting that Dublin Simon was in breach of the Planning Act 1963 – the Simon house was not an 'ordinary' family house, but a house of care with medical connotations.

As a result, representatives of Dublin Simon attended a meeting with city councillors, officials of the Health Board, and officials of the Planning Department, in the Dublin Corporation Offices in Dame Street. They were cross-questioned on the use of the Melrose Avenue house. Was the house an end in itself or a means towards further integration into society? Did these people not have families of their own who could help them to reintegrate? How long were 'patients' kept in the house? Simon representatives stated that they were prepared to consider any action in order to counteract the fears of the neighbours. They accepted that there had been disturbances and were still worried as to what could be done to stop the noise getting through to other houses in the area. On the issue of noise, one member of Simon wondered if a rowdy, noisy family would have produced the same reaction from the Residents' Association. Mr O'Reilly of Dublin Corporation mentioned the Planning Act and how it stated that if there was 'a change of use' an application for planning permission must be made – this was irrespective of the objections of Associations. The Corporation would have to decide whether or not to enforce the law in this instance and in so doing they would be guided by their Law Agent. In fact, when questions and difficulties arose on this type of issue the matter was normally referred to the Minister for Local Government. And this was what did happen subsequently.

Meanwhile life continued in 36 Melrose Avenue. Two residents who had been responsible for most of the disturbances had been moved out of the house. One, a lovable old man who *was* noisy when drunk, moved into a flat with a few former Simon workers who were his friends. He continued to live with them until his death some years later. But the Fairview neighbours were still unhappy and were determined to pursue the matter. They did not accept the offer of a seat on the Management Committee of the house, nor did they wish to visit, when invited, for afternoon tea.

But some of them did co-operate with the *Sunday World* by telling their side of the story, which later resulted in an extraordinary piece of media coverage for Simon, headlined 'House of Horrors'. According to the report, set out in a luridly dramatic fashion, angry families attacked the Simon Community home, and told of drunkenness, drug-taking, violence, filthy language, fights and broken windows (*Sunday World*, 5 October 1975).

When, in October 1976, Mr Jim Tully, the then Minister for Local Government, without any consultation with Simon, decreed that the use intended by Simon for the Chapelizod house was 'development' and that there had been a change of use which required planning permission, the Simon Committee realised that the Fairview Residents' Association would also take advantage of this loophole in the law. Frank O'Leary describes the subsequent events which led to Simon being told by a High Court judge that they were running a 'hotel':

> During 1977, the new Planning Board, presided over by a District Justice, was set up. The Planning Department of the Corporation now changed their description of the Fairview house from being a 'hostel' to being 'a house of care'. An Bord Pleanála decided in October 1977 that this was development and required planning permission. At that stage the Committee intended applying for planning permission. Later, however, we got advice which our solicitor supported that we should not apply for planning permission but should let the Corporation sue us. It was thought that we would get a fairer hearing in Court than we would get from the Planning Board. So the final date passed and we did not make our application. Almost immediately, we got official warning from 'the Right Honourable the Lord Mayor, Aldermen, and Burgesses of Dublin' that legal proceedings would be taken against us. We wrote to every one of the City Councillors telling them what their Planning Department were doing in their name. Only two bothered to contact us.
>
> The court hearing was fixed for the 9th June, but that was adjourned by agreement to 7th July. On that occasion Junior Counsel, Vivian Lavan (who appeared free of charge)

had some difficulty in getting an adjournment to September. Mr Lavan wanted time to prepare his brief. While doing this he consulted Senior Counsel Mr T.G. Connolly, and then the bomb fell. In August Mr Connolly gave it as his opinion that Simon is an institution and that there was therefore a change of use at 36, Melrose Avenue. At the next court hearing on 1st September, Mr Lavan put up as brave a fight as he could. We tried to get a definition of a 'house of care'. The judge kept saying we were running a hotel! But he found us guilty and fined us £1.

The present [1978] position is that we have written promise from the Corporation that 'in view of our assurances that we are endeavouring to find alternative accommodation . . . the Planning Department is prepared to defer further legal action . . . until after Christmas (1978). However, it is essential (they remind us) that the house be run in such a manner that it will not cause problems to the local residents'.

(Dublin Simon Community, *Annual General Report*, 1977)

As has been noted, the last four Simon residents did not leave Melrose Avenue until May 1981. In the meantime Dublin Simon had done its utmost to find alternative accommodation. In August 1978 negotiations had begun towards the purchase of a house at 35 Seán MacDermott Street. The house, which needed to be reconstructed, adjoined the existing Simon house on that street. By November 1979, the Executive Committee in their new-found wisdom, had secured the necessary planning permission. Because of the extent of the reconstruction necessary, they once again contacted the Corporation in the hope of obtaining the use of a temporary house for four residents and two workers. They were aware that prosecution was yet again hanging over their heads. The housing section of the Corporation was unable to provide them with temporary housing.

In September 1980 a further court case was heard, but Dublin Simon got a stay of execution until the middle of 1981. By that time they had shaken the dust of Melrose Avenue off their shoes. But they did not allow their eviction to go unnoticed. On Saturday, July 4th 1981, they staged a protest march, which incorporated street theatre, to highlight their rejection in three areas of Dublin over a seven-year period. The areas in question were Ballymun, Chapelizod and Fairview. In the Catholic tradition, the age of seven is accepted as that age when a child has reached the use of reason; he or she is then supposed to know the difference between right and wrong. Over a seven-year period, the Dublin Simon Community had also come to the use of reason; they now understood the Planning Act 1963 and 1976, and they had learned that integration of homeless people into Dublin suburbia would not work.

6

DECISIONS AND DIRECTIONS

Shelter rules OK

In the early eighties, many of the volunteers in Dublin Simon talked about the 'Shelter' on Sarsfield Quay as though it had always existed. They spoke of certain residents as having lived in the 'Shelter' for thirteen years, but the residents themselves told a different story. They knew that Dublin Simon did not have a night shelter from the beginning. And they had their own views about the early years in the community houses on the Quay. When Anton Wallich-Clifford developed the idea of the tier system he had seen Night Shelters and Houses of Hospitality as forming the first tier. A House of Hospitality operated on a twenty-four hour basis. Residents could stay in during the day if they wished. The Dublin Simon house in Winetavern Street was a House of Hospitality; a core-group of residents was living there permanently, and there were full-time workers. Later on in Dublin Simon, this kind of house became known as a 'wet house'. When the Community moved from Winetavern Street to Sarsfield Quay in 1971, the two houses on the Quay operated as community houses. No 9 was a dry house and was run on a therapeutic community basis. No 10 was a wet house – home for a group of men and women who continued to have a steady pattern of heavy drinking.

There was no Night Shelter in Dublin Simon during that early period. But there was a growing awareness among workers and Committee members that a Night Shelter should be part of the Simon service. A Night Shelter, by definition, does not stay open during the day. Usually catering for large numbers, it closes in order to allow for adequate cleaning as well as the preparation of an evening meal. It sets out to provide food, shelter and companionship, free of charge, for men and women who have nowhere else to go at night. Shelters normally open around 7 pm and close after breakfast around 9 am. Dublin Simon workers in the early seventies often went to workshops and conferences in England where they met other volunteers from Simon-type organisations. They tended to return to Ireland convinced of the need to set up a Simon Night Shelter in Dublin.

There were many valiant attempts made to find a suitable premises, but all of no avail. The Dublin workers were becoming aware of homelessness as an issue. They reckoned that they were, to some degree, meeting the needs of the men and women who were living permanently in the houses on the Quay. But the houses were virtually full. As Simon became better known, more and more people began to come to Sarsfield Quay in the hope of a cup of tea and a bed for the night. It was impossible to cope with the numbers even if all some people wanted was a chair for the night in the kitchen of No 10. The Executive Committee authorised the workers to give out a number of 'notes' per night for the Iveagh Hostel, in an effort to deal with the situation. (A 'note' entitled the homeless man to a bed in the Iveagh Hostel at the expense of Dublin Simon.) But this was not a satisfactory solution. The Iveagh was an expensive hostel and even six 'notes' per night added up to a sizeable bill at the end of each week. The Simon workers grew more and more convinced that some effort should be made to set up even a mini Night Shelter.

When the soup-run headquarters moved from the Quay to Harcourt Street in January 1972, there was a ground-floor front room free in No 10. It was decided that the ten or so beds in this room should be reserved for 'casuals', people who came looking for a bed for the night. It was to operate on a Night Shelter basis, the people being expected to leave by a certain time in the morning. Efforts were also made by some of the workers to ascertain why some of these newcomers were homeless. In some cases they were referred to other services which were better suited to their needs. In the case of teenagers, their parents or their social workers were usually contacted. So the beginning of a Night Shelter co-existed for some time alongside the boisterous community life of No 10. By the autumn of 1973 the Night Shelter had taken over the whole of No 10. The No 9 residents had moved to Northumberland Square and the wet house was operating in No 9. The 1973 Annual General Report comments on this development:

> With the residents gone, extra space was available in the Shelter for more expansion. There are now 30 beds in the Night Shelter, an increase of nearly 100%. Here men and women who would otherwise be sleeping rough are provided with a bed, food and companionship. Many of them are making their first contact with Simon. Casework with these people reveals a great variety of problems, some of them soluble. All are provided with medical attention, clothes and advice on social welfare problems. They have a real opportunity if they wish it, to begin moving up the Simon structure to a dry level.

In the course of 1974 the Night Shelter in No 10 continued to operate alongside the community house in No 9. Successive groups of full-time workers came and went; each had its own view of how the Shelter should be run. In accounts of life in the Quay which appeared in *Link* and in policy documents dating from this period, words such as 'revitalisation' and 'reorganisation' keep cropping up. A great effort was being made to ensure that life for the residents and the casuals in the Shelter was as pleasant as possible. But there was also a great deal of inconsistency as regards policy, because of the constant turnover of workers.

The reiteration in 1973 of the Committee's decision not to admit anyone in the 'under 40' age group to the Night Shelter, was a major bone of contention. There were valid reasons behind this decision. A number of younger people – some in their teens, others in their twenties – had lived in the Simon houses in the earlier years. In the first two years Simon had seen itself as a kind of 'catch-all' for anyone who needed shelter. But it became obvious to Committee members, many of whom were former workers, that Simon was a stepping stone downwards rather than upwards for younger people. It was, however, the full-time workers and co-workers who had to implement the 'under 40' decision, and not all of them were fully behind it.

In the latter half of 1974 much of the energy of the Executive Committee was devoted to finding alternative housing for those residents who had been living in Northumberland Square. The Committee also tended to be indecisive during this period, having lost Frank Sweeney and Bob Cashman from among their ranks. While there was an awareness of the needs of the Shelter, the Committee had little time or energy to devote to the detailed consideration of such needs. It was probably around this period that the tension in Dublin Simon between shelter work and the running of residential houses began to emerge. This tension has continued to exist.

Early in 1975 a day-long discussion was held in an attempt to define policy. Committee members, workers and co-workers were present. The needs of the Night Shelter were again considered. A decision was made to move some of the residents from 9 Sarsfield Quay into the house in Dorset Street, where a 'wet' community already existed, as a result of the move from Northumberland Square in 1974. A considerable amount of renovation work had been carried out in Dorset Street, and it was now to become the one official wet house of the Community. The Night Shelter was to be extended into No 9 to allow for greater comfort rather than for more people.

This emphasis on the need for a full-scale Shelter was accompanied by a desire to pay more attention to 'casework' and 'referral work'. From a social worker's point of view, casework means studying each individual client, keeping records of interviews, and discussing with the client himself and with other professional team members how best the client may be helped. Referral work involves making decisions as to whether a client should be referred to another helping agency, or perhaps be directed towards a different living situation. Originally Dublin Simon did not have an explicit commitment to this kind of an approach, because it appeared to contradict its emphasis on non-judgemental acceptance. But at the policy meeting in 1975 a decision was made to employ a professional social worker, precisely because the Executive Committee felt that proper referral work should be carried out in the Shelter.

A more professional approach

Over the years attempts had been made in Dublin Simon to do casework with individual residents. A few of the full-time workers had studied social work and were aware of the need to keep written records on the residents. Some workers had also seen the need to differentiate between the different kinds of people who came to the Night Shelter on a casual basis; some needed the kind of basic care that Simon could provide, while others needed a referral service. Any attempts, however, to do individual casework, or to provide a referral service, were piecemeal up until 1975. It all depended on what full-time workers, or co-workers, were around at the time. Records were not kept consistently. Individual residents grew tired of being interviewed by yet another full-time worker, who in their view, had not been 'a wet day in the Simon'. Valuable contacts with statutory agencies and voluntary organisations were lost because of the constant turnover of full-time workers. The response of the Executive Committee to this state of affairs was its decision to employ a qualified social worker who, they hoped, would lend an air of professionalism to the work being done by Dublin Simon.

Not every social worker would have been able to cope with Simon-type work. The Executive Committee were prepared to pay their prospective employee according to the social workers' salary scale of the day. They were looking for someone with a flexibility of approach, who would be able to take stock of the situation in Dublin Simon. John Long, the legendary full-time worker from the Winetavern Street era, had just returned from London where he had spent some years working for Westminster City Council while acquiring a Certificate of Qualification in Social Work (C.Q.S.W.). He was an obvious choice and he took up office with Dublin Simon in August 1975. He had the immediate advantage of knowing the long-term Simon residents. He had as well that natural ability to work with homeless people, a vital quality for anyone trying to do individual casework with Simon residents. The Simon Community to which he returned had expanded greatly. In his time all the Community members would have known each other, and administration, which was kept to a minimum, had been done by full-time workers.

In 1975 he returned to quite a sophisticated organisational structure. The administration work was being done by a team of paid staff. The soup-run continued and depended solely on co-workers. A follow-up team had been established. This group, who visited Simon residents in hospital and in prison, also drew its members from among co-workers. The Simon shop was functioning well and making a major contribution to Community funds. Most important of all, perhaps, Simon was beginning to develop a housing policy, which made a clear distinction between Night Shelter accommodation and residential houses. There were three residential houses in August 1975 – Dorset Street, Harcourt Street and Fairview. On the Quay, preparations were under way for a major renovation job, which would produce a Shelter with six large bedrooms, an extended kitchen-cum-dining room, an office, a medical room, a clothes store, toilets and showers. Full-time workers were being recruited through the National Office.

John Long set about his task in a systematic fashion. He visited the residential houses regularly to chat with the residents and was available in the Harcourt Street office for a couple of hours daily. But it was to the Shelter that he gave most of his energy during the early months of his employment. He was keen to interview everyone who used the Shelter, in order to build up a picture of the case histories and needs of the individual casuals and residents. In order to do this effectively, he decided to be available in the Shelter between 8 am and 10 am from Monday to Friday of each week. This was the time of the day when people were ready to talk. They had had a night's rest, and breakfast, and above all they were sober. John's priorities were firstly, to see that anyone who should not be in the Shelter would be moved on as quickly as possible, whether into a bedsitter, a hostel or a living situation provided by some other agency, and secondly, to ensure that those who would continue to use the Shelter would be as comfortable as possible. This meant sorting through certain problems in relation to healthcare, or clothing, or finance.

In the course of his interviews both in the Shelter and in the residential houses, John came up with three basic skeleton stories, the bones of which made up the case histories of many of the men who relied on Dublin Simon. They went something like this.

I'm over forty, unemployed and receiving unemployment

assistance. I've no skills or qualifications. I grew up in the inner city, was a member of a large family. We were poor, lived in overcrowded conditions and I didn't get much schooling. My father got casual work sometimes and my mother was a cleaning lady. I got into trouble and was sent to Artane or Daingean. I got into the army. Later on I went to England. When I came back my mates were all married. I used to get casual work but then I had to go on the labour. I started to drink to pass the time – I was staying in hostels. I ended up in jail for being drunk and disorderly.

I was born down the country. My father had a small holding. I didn't get much schooling. I used to do labouring work, then they got machinery. I went further afield, started to drink, couldn't talk easy to a woman. Then I went to England and I got good money there. When I came back I couldn't get a job. I had to go on the labour and stay in a hostel.

I'm on the old age pension. I go round from place to place. I've no family and I'm just passing the time. I like living in my own world and don't bother to have nothing to do with nobody. I do what I want and go where I want. I've been in mental hospitals and I get peace and quiet there.

(*Simon Ireland Newsletter*, June, 1976)

By this time Dublin Simon was also benefiting from a professional medical back-up service. Alice Leahy, an experienced nurse, had been a full-time worker on the Quay in 1973. Then in her thirties, she had a mature, practical approach to the needs of the residents. Of medium height, her strength of character showed in her facial features and in her tone of voice. Having finished her spell of full-time work on the Quay, she took up the post of Assistant National Co-ordinator and worked with Dick Shannon in the National Office for a year. Part of her work with Simon Ireland involved researching and compiling a report called 'Medical Care for the Vagrant' which was distributed to hostels, day centres and to other agencies. This report, published by Simon Ireland in 1974, highlighted the position of hostel dwellers and those sleeping rough with regard to medical care. Hostel staff told of a high incidence of respiratory, urinary and digestive problems. Malnutrition was also a matter of concern, and vagrants naturally suffered greatly from foot complaints. Only two of the nine Dublin Hostels surveyed had a visiting doctor, and many hostel dwellers did not have medical cards. Hospitals in the Dublin area received questionnaires.

> Replies included a concerned response from the Medical Administrator at St James Hospital which best expressed the general feeling among medical staffs of interest in the problem of the vagrant.
>
> At the other end of the scale the response from another city hospital showed the depth of intolerance encountered, at times, by the vagrant in his search for medical care. Here the casualty officer felt his main problem dealing with vagrants was 'smell'. The sister in charge of the casualty department said no dole money should be given to vagrants and believed some of them were too pampered with food, clothes and accommodation!
>
> (*Medical Care for the Vagrant in Ireland*, Dublin, 1974)

The Eastern Health Board accepted many of the recommendations in this report and in March 1975 they employed Alice with the brief of developing a medical service relevant to the needs of the homeless. She was joined by voluntary workers – among them Dave Magee, who as a medical student had also been a full-time worker on the Quay. Meanwhile money became available from an unusual source to develop further the service on a formal basis. Anne Rushe, a married woman with a young family, had been a soup-runner with Simon from the early days. In 1975 she became aware that she was suffering from a terminal illness. Having heard about the efforts that were being made to develop an appropriate medical service for vagrants she decided to make some money available for this cause. This money was used to establish the organisation, 'Trust'.

'Trust' came into being in November 1975, as a result of a lot of work and discussion by a number of individuals. In addition to Alice Leahy and Dave Magee, the founding members were Bob Cashman, Dermot McMahon, Justin O'Brien, John Long, Owen Mulholland and Anne Rushe herself. All of these, with the exception of Owen Mulholland, a solicitor, were or had been members of Simon. They became the original trustees and were joined by an additional member who represented the Eastern Health Board. Anne Rushe continued to give the organisation every possible support and encouragement until her death in March 1976.

The aim of 'Trust' was clearly stated:

> . . . to serve homeless people in need by promoting human services to meet their immediate and longterm needs and thereby to encourage their development and bring a rightful dignity to their lives.
>
> (*Simon Ireland Newsletter*, January, 1978)

By January 1976 Dave Magee, now a qualified doctor, had been employed full-time by 'Trust'. Dave, in his mid-twenties, had a genial manner and always appeared to be in good humour. During his term as a Simon full-time worker he had got on well with residents and workers alike. He and Alice both possessed that natural quality, as did John Long, of being able to relate in a friendly yet respectful manner with the homeless population of Dublin. Alice was now seconded to 'Trust' by the Eastern Health Board who also provided premises at the Health Centre in Lord Edward Street. John Long, who was employed by Simon, gave a considerable amount of time to 'Trust' from January 1976. He had discovered by this time that there was not really a full-time job for a social worker within Dublin Simon, so he was happy with his dual function which brought him into contact with all aspects of homelessness.

This 'Trust' team of nurse, doctor, and social worker spent two-thirds of their time directly with clients at the hostels, in the day centres, and in the Lord Edward Street health centre. One third of their time was spent in contact with statutory and voluntary agencies on behalf of the clients' immediate and long-term needs. This co-operative, professional approach to the medical needs of the homeless had an immediate spin-off for Dublin Simon, especially in the Shelter. Alice, Dave and John were available in the Shelter a couple of times a week, and were on call at any time. Systematic attention was paid to the health needs of the residents and the casuals. In the past residents had received medical attention in crisis situations; now the stress was on the every-day chronic ailments from which many homeless people suffer constantly on account of their lifestyle. Such ailments needed specific medical attention from time to time. But, above all, improved living conditions with adequate attention being paid to hygiene, nutrition, warmth and ventilation were vital in order to improve the health of the individual homeless man or woman. Prevention was more important than cure. *Link*, the *Simon Ireland Newsletter* and the Annual General Report of 1976 all testify to this new awareness among members of Dublin Simon. On 28 February 1976, a 'Shelter Seminar' organised by Justin O'Brien, was held in Buswell's hotel. Justin O'Brien opened the seminar with a talk on the history of the Shelter.

> He said that when the No. 9 residents moved to Dorset Street it was the first time that the Shelter stood solely as a Night Shelter. He said that when the builders were finished he would like to see people considering the place as a brand new Shelter – not just physically but especially in the quality of the service offered.
>
> Alice and Dave talked about 'health' in the broadest meaning of the word. Alice emphasised the importance of 'soap and water' and said that there is no point in having the place smelling of disinfectant if it is still dirty.
>
> Dave said that the quality of the food should be improved. He said that the tinned soup had little nourishment and that it should be sufficiently reinforced by whatever vegetables and bones might be available. A little Complan should also be put in the soup.
>
> Dave went on to criticise the attitude of the person who treats the visitor to the Shelter like a 'strange being' and who would present him with food which they would not dream of touching themselves. He asked if this was the way one should treat one's brother or sister if they should end up in a Simon Shelter.
>
> Alice suggested that towels could be made from the backs of old shirts and she said they should always be available in the Shelter. There should always be a supply of clean shirts and socks and the local laundry have offered drying facilities, so washing clothes should not be such a problem.

In the course of his talk John Long spoke on the subject of referral. The funny thing is, he said, that most people who wanted a flat simply went out and got one for themselves. This gives rise to the question, on whom should we be forcing referral and why? John said that we tend to pick on men who have managed to pick themselves up a little and who keep themselves a little better than most others in the Shelter. There is a tendency, therefore, to victimise people who have simply used the Shelter to its full advantage, but who could fail totally in another situation. A situation like a flat, for example.

John suggested that there was a huge cultural divide between the average co-worker and casual. Because of this, our relationships tend to be on the shallow side. We could never, for example, have the same relationship with a casual that two casuals could have between themselves. Relating this to follow-up on people who get a flat, our visits can be pleasant and helpful to the person but we could hardly remove the emptiness that person feels by being alone. The ideal situation would be where a few people live together in a flat or in a group of flats in the same house, where they would operate their own natural, group-support system. Another point which John commented on was the co-workers' 'compulsion to do things'. He emphasised the value of 'just being there' as a concerned person, prepared to listen, but not feeling obliged to maintain a conversation.

It was agreed by all at the seminar that after the renovation work the House Management should meet with the people who use the Shelter to hear their views and to discuss new plans.

(*Link*, February/March, 1976)

The year 1976 proved to be exhausting for the decision makers in Dublin Simon. Justin O'Brien, as Chairman, was not only involved in clarifying policy in relation to the Shelter, he was also to the fore right through the crisis over the house in Chapelizod. The work of the Executive Committee was only made possible by the consistent back-up they had from an excellent administration team. Frank O'Leary was still at the helm, dealing with all the nitty-gritty of the day-to-day responsibility for the Community. Paul Harrison continued to do invaluable work in relation to the recruitment, training and co-ordination of the co-worker force. Annette Kavanagh, a sister of a former full-time worker, looked after the secretarial work. To add even more stress to the situation, Dublin Simon had to start looking for alternative office space, on account of having to vacate the house in Harcourt Street.

Community or organisation?

The house in Harcourt Street, which Dublin Simon had acquired on a caretaker's agreement in January 1972, had fulfilled many purposes over the years. Georgian in style, with four floors and a basement, it provided valuable space in a central location. By the middle of 1976, when the Community finally had to vacate the premises, it was being used for three separate areas of Simon work. The soup-run operated from the basement, which contained basic equipment such as a cooker and a sink. On the top floor, in a self-contained flat, five quiet residents lived with a couple of workers. From the first floor could be heard the hustle and bustle of telephones and typewriters; here, in three rooms, operated the administration team of Dublin Simon. The rooms, with their large Georgian windows, were bright and cheerful. The atmosphere was friendly. Former workers often dropped in to catch up on Community news. Full-time workers came down from 'upstairs' to use the phone. A cup of coffee was usually available for those in need. Harcourt Street was part of Dublin Simon; it was hard to imagine administration operating from another location. So it was a major blow for the Community, though not an unexpected one, when the caretaker's agreement came to an end in June 1976.

It is not possible to run an organisation efficiently if the administrative headquarters is not a permanent one. Dublin Simon had, in fact, been lucky with the house in Harcourt Street; it had provided them with good office accommodation, rent-free, for four and a half years. But now they were faced with an important decision. If they wanted security of tenure, they were going to have to pay for it.

The Executive Committee decided to rent a premises, at commercial rates, in the city centre. The new office was on the third floor of a premises just off Marlborough Street, and once again it contained three rooms – a large board room, a compact office for the Administrator, and an outer office for the Assistant and Secretary. There was no indication at the entrance to the building that it contained the Dublin Simon office. The thinking behind this was prompted by the nature of the relationship between administration and the residents and casuals who availed of the Simon service. As far as the Executive Committee was concerned, administration was precisely that, and must function in a professional manner. So they did not want homeless people calling to the office. Individual Executive members and administrative staff visited the Shelter and the residential houses regularly, but they were not keen on these visits being returned. With the move to Marlborough Place, where the Dublin Simon offices are still located, a clear distinction was drawn between Simon as organisation and Simon as community.

In the early years Simon had survived literally from day to day. There had been a common 'vision' among the members of the Community. This 'vision' was comfortably vague and it did not involve much hard planning; but it kept people going. On days off, over a few drinks, full-time workers talked excitedly about possible new projects – a therapeutic community for young people, a transitional house from which residents would move effortlessly back into society, a work project which would be all-encompassing and self-supporting. The enthusiasm and imagination and goodwill were marvellous, but there was a certain air of unreality about it all. The older, and consequently wiser, members of the Executive Committee kept a watchful eye over developments.

Gradually a little more structure crept in. The Northumberland Square crisis had brought the joint issues of policy and authority to the fore. With the resignation of Frank Sweeney and Bob Cashman, the remaining members of the Executive Committee were left with the final responsibility for the direction of the organisation. Justin O'Brien, then in his mid-twenties, had been a co-worker and a full-time worker before becoming an Executive member. Subsequently he served as vice-chairman for a year and as chairman for two years before leaving the Community in the autumn of 1977 to do a child-care course in Kilkenny. He told me that he and other members of the Committee found themselves trying to push through exactly the same kind of decisions that they might have opposed when Frank Sweeney and Bob Cashman were in the key positions. It is easy to be radical when in opposition; those on whom the final responsibility rests must be pragmatic and make some definite decisions.

The original sense of Dublin Simon as a community was based on a certain understanding of democracy, and on the famous founding principles of Simon which had been adapted for the Irish Communities (see Appendix 1). This understanding of democracy demanded that important decisions should be made by the Community as a whole, and that is what happened, to some degree at least, when Dublin Simon was small and centred on Sarsfield Quay. But this ideal became progressively more difficult to attain as the organisation grew. Despite the creation of House Management Committees and a Co-worker Council, each with their own representative on the Executive, there were many people in Dublin Simon who felt isolated and powerless when it came to influencing policy. The kind of democracy that gradually developed was that which obtains in the majority of organisations. Each year, at the Annual General Meeting, an Executive Committee was elected according to the rules laid down in the Articles of Association. This Committee then had the power to make decisions and be a guiding force on behalf of the organisation as a whole.

In such an organisation, the definition of membership is important, as only ordinary members have a right to vote at Annual General Meetings. This issue of membership first arose towards the end of 1974. The November issue of *Link* reports:

> Due to the quick turnover of co-workers and full-time workers, it has become necessary to introduce a system of membership. Before this we were able to define who was or wasn't a member of Simon. So after a lot of thought, the following was decided:
>
> 1. Full-time workers will automatically become Ordinary Members.
> 2. Co-workers will become Ordinary Members after two months in Simon; and they will remain so, provided they are not missing for more than two months without a reason. Ordinary members have a vote.

3. Ex full-time workers will become Associate members, and will not, therefore, have a vote.
4. People like Dr Gerry O'Neill and Pat Whelan who do much work for Simon will be offered Ordinary Membership.
5. Residents will become Ordinary Members.
6. Casuals have no membership rights.

A subscription of 50p will fall due for Ordinary Members, on 1st January 1975.

By the autumn of 1975 the rules had become more stringent. Again I quote from *Link*, the September 1975 issue:

The Annual General Meeting will be held sometime in November. The following is a list of points to remember in that connection.

1. *Only paid up members* will be allowed propose and vote.
2. Official forms will be sent to all paid up members. These will be for your written proposals for Committee members. These forms should be sent back to the office before the AGM.
3. Voting cards will also be sent to paid up members, and these cards should be brought along on the day of the AGM.
4. A list of present Committee members and other relevant details will be published in the next edition of 'Link'.

By the end of 1975 then, the issue of membership had been clarified. Unlike other organisations catering for the single homeless Simon made their long-term residents Ordinary Members of the Community. This, of course, stemmed from Anton Wallich-Clifford's original conviction that Simon should work *with* and not *for* the homeless. Residents should have a say in the running of the Community and eventually become workers or administrators if they showed an aptitude for such activities. This kind of idealistic approach did operate to some degree in Dublin Simon for the first couple of years, but gradually people were honest enough to admit that there had to be some clear dividing line between workers and residents. Certain responsibilities such as minding the keys to a safe which contained drugs, housekeeping money and other valuables had to be undertaken by workers. There was still a good deal of talk about identification, and workers and co-workers were anxious that the residents should have as much say as possible in the running of their own lives. And indeed the smaller units such as Fairview and Harcourt Street did manage to function as small, homely communities.

But once membership of the Community as a whole became an issue, this desire to be true to the Simon ideal was met by offering Ordinary Membership to the residents. In theory, it was a fair enough solution. In practice, however, it seemed to mean very little. With a few notable exceptions, residents rarely attended the Annual General Meetings. On one occasion a few of them turned up drunk and were a disruptive force. As a result it was agreed that no one who was drunk should be admitted to an AGM. The fact of the matter seems to be that Ordinary Membership of a community/organisation, which is structured in a formal manner, requiring written proposals and the use of voting cards, is hardly such a great gift to homeless people who are just not 'at home' with the sheer formality of such procedures.

By the middle of 1976, when administration moved from Harcourt Street to the new offices in Marlborough Place, Dublin Simon was already functioning both as a Community and as an organisation. Community life continued in the Shelter and in the residential houses through the ordinary daily interaction between residents, co-workers and workers. The same small crises developed, the same need for companionship and healing existed, and there was always the crack – the witty joke, the brilliant turn of phrase, the sheer good humour in the face of the struggle. Community of a different kind operated on the soup-run and on follow-up, where men and women who slept rough, or were in prison, or in hospital, looked forward to seeing their Simon friends on a regular basis. And Community operated on a wider level as former workers met and chatted and remembered good times.

But an organisational structure also existed in Dublin Simon. Committee members had had endless meetings with the Chapelizod Residents' Association, with Dublin Corporation, with the Eastern Health Board. Much effort had to be put into fund-raising as the Community had a steadily growing expenditure, largely due to the purchasing of houses and renovation work in the Shelter. Effort was needed in the area of public relations. While flexibility might have been the key word in Simon's approach to their residents, in administrative terms, efficiency was what really mattered.

Crisis in the Shelter

In his Chairman's report to the 1976 AGM, Justin O'Brien made the following comment:

> For the Committee it has been a demanding year as we were faced with the difficulty of Chapelizod. But our greatest difficulty has been that local project problems came to Executive level, thus diminishing the important planning function of an Executive Committee.

Justin's comment conjures up pictures of bleary-eyed Committee members, tired after a day's work, spending hours discussing issues relating to how the Shelter should be run, who should be barred and how to cope with the shortage of full-time workers. If 1976 proved a difficult year in this regard, the problems had not been solved by January 1st 1977. Around this time the Executive Committee had been discussing the possibility of employing a full-time salaried worker to act as Manager in the Shelter on the Quay. This person, according to the advertisement which appeared in the February 1977 edition of *Link*, would 'be responsible for the general running of the project, particularly the supervision of the full-time workers and co-workers, and the maintenance and general upkeep of the shelter'. The salary was in the region of £2,000 per annum and the person employed was to be required to work at least a forty-hour week which would include various unsocial hours.

This decision by the Committee elicited various responses from Community members. Some people felt strongly enough to write to *Link*. Peter Gahan, a former full-time worker in the Shelter and co-editor of *Link* during this period, used the *Newsletter* to write 'an open letter to the Committee'; he did not only tackle the issue in hand but spoke of his deeper fears about the direction being taken by Dublin Simon.

> Simon has been at the stage now (for the past three years)

> where it must make a decision. This decision (perhaps unfortunately undemocratic) must be made at Executive Committee level as they are the present decision-making body in Simon. The decision to make is simply a resolution not to make any decisions which are contradictory to Simon founding principles. Or, the Executive Committee can decide that they are satisfied with the way Simon has developed into a relatively inefficient hierarchical organisation in the past four or five years and so do nothing. They will probably do the latter.
>
> But immediately people will ask 'what founding principles?' . . . Founding principles are simply the way you find yourself working in Simon and whether you have some sense of 'vision' as to how the work should go . . . Which brings me to the issue at hand: the instituting of the institution of a Manager for the Quays. I do not want to go into this in detail because it is only one of a number of issues. However, it seems to me like an attempt by you, the Executive Committee, to exercise power and control where you have not been able to exercise it effectively before.
>
> What you must realise is that you are not Simon and it does not matter whether your control is effective in the Quays or not. What does matter is how life goes on down in the Quays and in that you can be a guiding force. The element of trust must not be broken and replaced by force (i.e., authority) . . . .
>
> (*Link*, February, 1977)

Peter's conclusion was that Dublin Simon needed to decide, once and for all, to 'stem the rot of bureaucratic structures' which had been 'fraudently introduced in the name of greater organisational efficiency'.

That same edition of *Link* (February, 1977) carried a letter from Frank O'Leary, then Secretary of the Executive Committee, in which he outlined some of the reasons for the contentious decision.

> . . . Now for a bit of more recent Shelter history. A few weeks ago the workers, following a majority decision, were removing some people from the Shelter. At the same time

a dissenting co-worker was re-admitting the same people through the other door! That is democracy gone mad and it is this two-door democracy that exasperates, drains and exhausts everybody. Last Friday Larry remarked: 'Nice and quiet down there now and that's the way we want it.' Any one of thirty other people who use the Shelter could echo those words. But then, maybe these weary old men do not know what's good for them. Someone will surely argue that chaos and bedlam keep their minds alert and more accessible to democratic principles!

Last week a full-time worker who had settled in very happily left rather suddenly. He saw himself becoming more and more a 'full-time bouncer'.

Also last week, a difficult, even dangerous, young casual turned up at the Shelter and nobody knew him. He had been in prison for a few months and in the meantime the entire full-time worker group had changed. In circumstances like this workers can be bullied, manipulated, conned and even exposed to physical danger . . . Multiply these incidents by five thousand and add in the lost keys, the blocked sewers, the broken cookers, and so on, and you will get a vague picture of Sarsfield Quay. In no way do I blame the workers, the present group (who, incidentally, are keeping the cleanest Shelter we ever had) or any previous groups. Things get lost, information gets lost, personalities clash, continuity breaks down and our Simon people are the ones to suffer from the ensuing confusion.

We have always stressed that the primary function of the Simon worker is to relate to our people; to listen, to heal, to love. The function of the Committee is to support the workers; to make available the houses, the money and whatever other supportive structures are necessary. They should also adapt to changing needs. It is very significant that all Committee members who have been involved with management of the Quays in the last two years are strongly in favour of the introduction of a full-time Manager. The Chairperson of the present Management Committee 'cannot wait' for his arrival.

The new Manager could be a hostel warden type. But it is not beyond the bounds of possibility that he could be a good leader who is able to get the best out of everybody

> with whom he is working. He could even make the Quays a more pleasant place to spend the night, a more peaceful place to work in . . .

Frank O'Leary made the point that one of the functions of the Committee was to provide whatever supportive structures were necessary to enable the workers to do a good job. When, in 1975, the Committee had decided to employ a professional social worker, they had hoped that this would be just such a supportive structure. The social worker appointed then, John Long, told me that in retrospect, it seemed to him that the Committee had hoped that a social worker would be able to wave a magic wand which would make all the problems disappear. This was not to be. John contributed greatly to Dublin Simon during his term of employment, which ended in December 1977. He afterwards served on the Executive Committee. But there was still a vacuum which could not be filled by the use of social work skills. By deciding to employ a Manager for the Shelter, Dublin Simon took an important step, which they have not so far regretted.

The late Conor O'Neill was the first person to fill that post. By May 1977 he had commenced work. Unfortunately his stay was a brief one. By the autumn of 1977 the Committee was again seeking a suitable person for the post. By this time the title had been changed to 'Project Leader'. Tommy Cooney, a long-term co-worker on the Quay, was chosen and by December 1977 he was officially installed as Project Leader in the Shelter. Almost immediately a new stability was evident. Tommy's experience and practical approach meant that policy once defined, was implemented with a firmness that made both residents and workers feel more secure.

7

NEW IDEAS, NEW VENTURES

A bird's-eye view

I visited the Dublin Simon offices in Marlborough Place on a number of occasions in the early months of 1983. The staff were both friendly and helpful, as I tried to put together the various pieces of the Dublin Simon jigsaw puzzle. Carmel Bradley, who was Administrator at the time, radiated warmth and vitality. A small woman in her early thirties, she had been working with Simon since the beginning of 1977; I gleaned much valuable information from listening to her reminiscences. She had started work with Dublin Simon at a time when there was a complete change of staff in administration. The office had moved to Marlborough Place in the middle of 1976. When, some months later, Frank O'Leary resigned, after a three-year stint as Administrator, Padraig O'Connor was appointed in his place. By this time a decision had been made to cut the administrative staff to two; Carmel was the successful applicant for the post of Secretary.

She remembered loving the job at the beginning. She had lived abroad for some years, and having decided to return to Ireland was keen to get an interesting job. Although the post in Dublin Simon was that of a low-paid secretary, it provided her with the kind of challenge she was seeking. She thought the workers were 'fabulous people'. She used to visit the Shelter and residential houses as a friend – over and above what was required by her job. By the end of 1977, she felt she had got the hang of things. Nevertheless the lack of continuity in the administration team had made itself felt in the course of the year. And the Committee was aware of the crucial role played by the full-time staff.

During the year we have had a complete change in our full-

> time staff. With such change naturally contacts and experiences are lost and greater burdens are placed on new staff. We have often expected our full-time staff to work long hours with little financial remuneration. Is it not time we changed our attitude and gave our staff a salary commensurate with their ability and status?
> (Dublin Simon Community, Annual General Report, 1977)

By April 1978 Padraig O'Connor had resigned from his position as Administrator. Austin Finnerty, a twenty-eight year old northerner, was appointed in his place. Carmel was promoted to the position of Assistant Administrator. Although she was still responsible for the bulk of the secretarial work, her new post significantly increased her level of responsibility. Her scope as secretary had been limited, and after the initial excitement the job had become a routine one. She now had her own distinct areas of administrative responsibility, such as liaising with the staff of the Simon shop and co-ordinating co-worker activities. Carmel told me that she loved challenge. She could have become bored with the position of Assistant Administrator also, and once or twice she was on the verge of leaving. But in April 1979 Austin Finnerty resigned from his position as Administrator. This kind of turnover in office staff was beginning to give cause for concern. Carmel had been working with Simon for over two years; she was familiar with most aspects of the Community.

In May 1979 she was appointed to the post of Administrator. She was becoming that most important of all commodities in Dublin Simon – a valuable continuity link. Meanwhile Frank O'Leary had been chairman of the Executive Committee since the autumn of 1977. So, as the Dublin Simon Community headed for the eighties, there was promise of continuity at both Executive and Administrative level.

The year 1980 was a significant one for Dublin Simon's attitude towards its 'paid staff'. This term did not only apply to those involved in administration; there were now salaried Project Leaders for the Shelter and for the residential house in Seán McDermott Street. Simon, while still availing itself of the commitment and enthusiasm of the short-term volunteer, realised the need for stable leadership in each of its projects. Tommy Cooney had done wonders for the Shelter since his employment began in December 1977. Meanwhile

Brendan McCarry, a former full-time worker, had in October 1979 been appointed as the first Project Leader in 36 Sean McDermott Street; eventually there was to be a second residential house adjoining this one, and both houses were to be seen as the one 'Project'. So Simon had a steadily growing salaried workforce. In 1980 several new appointments were made, and serious consideration was given to the question of financial remuneration.

> New status was also added this year to our method of making new staff appointments [said the Annual General Report for 1980]. Because we had adopted for the first time a proper salary scale, we were able to advertise witn a new confidence which was fully justified by the very high standard of applicants for the posts. We are very happy with – in fact we are proud of – the subsequent appointments made. They are – Cathy Power as Assistant Administrator; Teresa Connolly-Mukerjee as Project Leader in Seán McDermott Street, and Gerry Fulham as Project Leader in the Shelter. Tommy Cooney transferred from the Shelter to lead the new Work Project. We welcome the new appointees and wish them well.

In January 1981, the Executive Committee discussed the possibility of employing a third person to join the administrative team as an Education Officer. This issue of public education had been coming up again and again at policy meetings. Dublin Simon must, it was felt, communicate with the general public on behalf of the single homeless people with whom it was working. But there were not enough funds available to employ a third person on a full-time basis.

A compromise was reached. Evelyn Bracken, a former co-worker and Committee member, was employed as a part-time secretary. Until then the Assistant Administrator, Cathy Power, had attended to this side of the work. She now continued to do the accounts and look after the co-ordination of co-workers, and she began to develop the educational aspect of Simon work. This meant circularising various voluntary organisations and schools asking permission for a Simon member to address their members or students. It also involved setting up stalls in Trinity College, University College Dublin, and St Patrick's Training College, Drumcondra, during their respective Freshers' Weeks. Such work proved time-consuming and required enthusiasm and determination, as the results of strenuous effort were not always immediately visible. On this front Dublin Simon worked in close connection with the National Office, which continued its campaign on behalf of the homeless.

Carmel Bradley, as Administrator, had a great deal of responsibility. Her position was a complex one. On the one hand she was responsible for the ordinary everyday management of the Community. Full-time worker welfare, negotiations over property, working alongside a financial adviser in order to plan the yearly budget, insurance problems, liaising with the Project Leaders – all these diverse tasks fell within the Administrator's terms of reference. On the other hand Carmel was answerable to the Executive Committee. Issues had to be thrashed out at Committee meetings which she attended regularly, and any really important decisions were taken at this level.

Despite the pressures she appeared to enjoy her job very much. The atmosphere in the office was one of friendliness and quiet efficiency, and the three staff members worked well as a team. When I asked Carmel about the high points of Simon life during her years of employment, she spoke with real delight about the camping holidays for the residents, which had been initiated by Tommy Cooney. She saw the establishment of the two houses in Sean McDermott Street as a sign of the mature and realistic approach which Dublin Simon had developed towards long-term residential housing. She worried about the fact that a lot of money was being wasted in the maintenance of the two houses on Sarsfield Quay, because the establishment of a new Shelter was proving so difficult. And above all she spoke about the Work Project and the difference it had made to the Community as a whole.

A dream come true

I set out to visit the Work Project on Sarsfield Quay on a damp February afternoon. As I walked down the quays from O'Connell Bridge I remembered some of the efforts that had been made in the previous decade to engage the Simon residents in some kind of work. In the early days workers maintained fiercely that 'Simon did not overtly aim at rehabilitation'. No one seemed to know precisely what they meant by this statement, but there was an air of sacredness about the principle behind it that few would have dared to challenge. As time went by people did begin to question such an approach. Some of the residents took the law into their own hands by getting casual work under their own steam and eventually moving away from Simon into Corporation flats or good 'squats' in various parts of the city.

But for those who continued to live full-time in Dublin Simon houses boredom was a real problem. At one point full-time workers organised candle-making; the end products were sold at a stall in the Dandelion Market, but when irate customers returned claiming that many of the larger candles only burned for one hour, that particular venture fell through. Then there was the field behind the old Kenilworth Cinema that was going to be turned into a market garden. And there was the workshop in Northumberland Square which had all kinds of possibilities. Somehow or other none of the ventures lasted for very long. But veteran members of Simon continued to have a dream; they hoped that one day they would be able to offer paid employment to at least some of their residents. 1980 was the year when the dream became a reality.

As a result of the planning meeting in January of that year, it was estimated that it would cost £54,000 to launch a Work Project and run it for one year. The kind of venture that Simon envisaged was a large workyard, in which glass, wood and old clothes could be recycled. Simon residents, both from the Shelter and Sean McDermott Street would be invited to work in the yard; they would be paid a daily rate, plus a bonus if they worked a five day week. The yard would be under the management of a Project Leader and a full-time worker. In addition, it was hoped to set up a laundry, complete with automatic washer and dryer, which would deal with the laundry from the Shelter and residential houses, as well as doing contract work for other voluntary organisations. It was decided that Simon should put £15,000 into the project themselves and that they would apply to the Inner City Fund for further financial aid. To their astonishment and delight a grant of £32,000 was approved in July 1980.

Meanwhile Dublin Corporation also co-operated by providing a yard at Ellis Place, which backed onto the Sarsfield

Quay Shelter, the necessary materials to build a wall around the area (50 yards long, 10 feet high), and two gates to enclose it. Some of the grant money was then used to purchase a pick-up truck, a chain-saw, and the machinery and tools necessary for the recycling of glass. The development of the laundry, which was to be located in the basement of one of the Sean McDermott Street houses, was not undertaken until the middle of 1981.

Tommy Cooney was the original Leader of the Work Project. While managing the Shelter he had already organised a number of the residents into a small work group, which was responsible for maintenance work in the Shelter. Tommy had been a co-worker with Simon for many years. A tradesman himself, he had an excellent relationship with the residents and was able to share his skills with them. He saw, too, the need for fun and relaxation. By May of 1981, the core-group of workers on the Project had enjoyed two weekends away together; these outings had been financed by the contributions of the workers themselves. In the 1981 Annual General Report, Tommy gives his own account of developments on the Project.

> The main developments in the Work Project this year [1981] were the appointment of a full-time driver and the start of the laundry. Johnny Walker is very welcome. He fitted in fine. It was also decided to reduce the work force from the twenty-six originally planned to thirteen. We work five days at collecting, sorting and breaking glass; at chopping and packaging kindling wood for sale to retail outlets and selling old clothes to a rag merchant. For a time our people enjoyed dining in a cafe near the Shelter, but to save money we now cook our own and dine in the yard. We had full-time workers on and off without any continuity. Electricity providing light and power for the saw has just been installed by the Corporation. In January, 20,000 leaflets about the Project, and inviting people to give us their glass, were distributed through schools in the north city. The press were invited to see us in action in March but only the Irish Press turned up and produced an article. In May, the Sunday World carried an article and some pictures. Still the voluntary delivery of bottles to the project is very poor.
>
> The original grant of £32,000 is finished since September,

but the Executive had no hesitation in deciding to keep the project going.

The greatest joy for me is to work closely with our people. For all the hard work they put into this project, I thank them very much. We had some great nights and some great weekends together.

The Work Project, however, began to give cause for concern on the financial front in the course of 1982. Frank O'Leary, still chairman of the Executive Committee, sums up the situation in the Annual General Report for that year.

A lot of time and discussion was given to this Project during the year. More than ever we are convinced of its social/therapeutic value, but the finance is a headache . . . .

The original grant given by the Department of the Environment (via the Inner City Fund) to set up the Project ran out in September 1981. From there on we had to finance it from Simon funds. Before Christmas we were dissatisfied with some aspects of the management of the project. This dissatisfaction was conveyed to the Project Leader at the time. At our Planning meeting in January we were very seriously concerned about the cost of the project. It transpired that it would cost about £30,000 for the year while the income would be only £9,000. We decided to allocate a maximum of £17,000 and that we would review the entire situation after three months.

During those months there were many discussions and suggestions. It was proposed to the Project Leader that he might accept redundancy. In February he expressed interest and some enthusiasm for this proposal. He said that after leaving Simon he intended doing the same type of work with some of the same people and he would be more free. Resulting from this development, a significant proposal was made: that the Shelter and the Work Project should be brought closer together so that the people 'on the dry' in the Shelter should feel free and be encouraged to work for even half a day in the week if they so wished and that ideally the two projects should be under one Leader with an Assistant. This idea was discussed and accepted at Executive level and on April 5th it was decided to make Tommy Cooney redundant.

Tommy Cooney finished as an employee with Dublin Simon in May 1982. Gerry Fulham, who had been Project Leader in the Shelter since June 1980, took on responsibility for the Work Project and Shelter as a combined venture. He was assisted by full-time worker Basil Leonard, who was subsequently appointed to the post of driver, when Johnny Walker left. Emphasis was once again laid on what had been the initial objective of the Work Project – to help relieve the boredom of the men and women who wanted to stay on the dry. In *Link* (June/July 1982) Basil Leonard gives us a picture of life in the yard:

> The month of May has basically been a period of rebuilding. Rebuilding has consisted of clearance of rubble, maintenance, etc. and most important of all in my opinion, the construction of THE DOOR, the entrance leading from the Shelter into the yard. This simple piece of engineering and architecture has broken down many barriers. Positive progress has been made in unifying the two . . . .
>
> Over the past month we have developed a reasonably consistent workforce. Teamwork is the order of the day and in this field I would like to think we have been successful. The ultimate achievement in work is to enjoy it. It's fun and should be enjoyed.
>
> Without over-praising, I must now look at the Work Project on a realistic level and put it in perspective. As regards the sticks, we are stockpiling for the winter – we have absolutely no sale for them at the moment. They are 'money in the bag' so to speak. They are a worthwhile proposition, but are somewhat tedious and time-consuming. Bottles are our chief money-spinner. At the moment we are only getting about half the amount of bottles we could consume. If we could double our intake of bottles, then we would clearly be in a position to break even or even make a profit. We think the answer lies in advertising and a more vigorous and sustained effort in collecting.
>
> Finally, I would like to say we are open to suggestions and ideas from everyone. Please drop down and pay us a visit, stay for a cup of tea, everyone is welcome. Of course, don't forget the few empty bottles when you come.

Unfortunately I forgot to bring the empty bottles the day

I visited the yard. But my welcome was no less warm for that omission. I met Gerry Fulham in the kitchen of the Shelter, where we had a mug of tea together. Gerry was still in his twenties, a dark-haired, burly young man with an easy manner and an air of confidence about him. He enjoyed working for Simon, but pointed out that it involved unsocial hours which might not suit him at all if he were married. Before bringing me out to the yard, he explained that the Work Project was still operating at a loss, but he seemed confident that with time and effort it would be possible to make it break even. He felt that the life-style of those working in the yard had improved greatly, and he hoped that it would be possible to expand the choice of work available to them in the future.

It was damp and windy outside. One end of the yard was protected from the elements by roofing. In this area one woman and a few men were working – chopping wood. They all agreed that they enjoyed the work. There was a real air of comradeship among them. One man, a resident from Seán McDermott Street, showed me some photos of their recent camping holiday. Molly, the only woman in the yard that day, told me that she had lived in the Shelter for a while, but now she had a room of her own. Tommy, who had a northern accent, explained that they got £3.00 a day and a bonus of £5.00 at the end of the week if they had worked a full week. A couple of the men made comments about this system of payment. It was terrible, they said, if you lost your fiver for only missing one day – the difference between £12.00 and £20.00 for the week.

Up at the other end of the yard I chatted with a couple of the men who were working with the glass. The first job involved was that of sorting the bottles. The returnable ones were precious, an immediate source of cash. All the other bottles had to be sorted according to colour, different colours going into separate barrels, and then the real fun began. The bottles and jars had to be smashed into pieces before being sold to a glass bottle factory. Matty, one of the champion bottle smashers, told me he loved the work. Since he started in the yard he had managed to rent a little room of his own. He liked to listen to his transistor there, in peace and quiet. And for the moment he was managing to stay off the drink. Matty had a religious outlook on life. He felt God was looking after him. His main regret in life was that he had caused his family so much trouble because of his drink problem. But things were looking up now. If he could stay off the booze, continue to work, and hold on to his little room, there was nothing more he could ask for. He wished me well and hoped the book about Simon would be a success.

There was no one working on the rags that day, but I could see mounds of old clothes piled in another corner of the yard. One of the men complained about the fact that they did not get enough bottles to keep them going. They could do with any amount, he said. While they had a truck, and a driver to do collections, it would be nice if people would deliver their old bottles – after Christmas, for example. I was struck by the interest the workers had in the project as a whole. They were obviously proud of their work and were anxious that the venture should be a success financially. I met Gerry again as I was leaving and I enquired about the laundry. He advised me to visit the Seán McDermott Street project and have a chat with the men who worked there.

Home at last

Dublin Simon now owns two adjoining houses in Seán McDermott Street – 35 and 36. The first of these houses, 36, was purchased in September 1976, when it became obvious, as a result of the hostility experienced in Chapelizod, that the Simon Community and the Dublin suburbs were not marriageable partners. By Christmas of that year it had been renovated and ten elderly residents moved there from the temporary house in Dorset Street. The second house, 35 Seán McDermott Street, was actually bought in June 1979: the first residents, however, did not move in until May 1981, by which time the necessary planning permission had been obtained and the bulk of the renovation work had been completed. From the outset, each of the Seán McDermott Street houses was seen as a residential house. The original residents in 36 were all elderly people; they needed care and comfort; most of them are now dead. But others came to take their places. And they did so, knowing that this was not a shelter-type house.

When Simon first moved into the area, they gave an undertaking to their neighbours that the house would be a quiet one and that residents would not drink on the street in the immediate vicinity of the house. The accepted Simon policy for the project was that it should be a peaceful house for older or enfeebled residents. Some of the residents, however, who moved into the house from the Shelter did not fit into that scheme of things. They proved disruptive. When challenged, they did not appear to be willing, or able, to modify their conduct. The dilemma which resulted, led, in the course of 1979, to much internal conflict on the essence of Simon policy. Yet again, those Simon principles were called upon by some. Members of the Executive Committee were accused of being heartless and of not really understanding the residents concerned. The Annual General Report of that year has many references to that conflict.

> Whether to re-admit a former resident, who was unable to cope in her flat, back to the house or not, caused a considerable amount of conflict among workers and co-workers in early summer. The division was a sharp and fairly basic one; it centred not so much on concrete difficulties as on differences of principle regarding the best way to treat residents. The conflict also brought into the open, difference of opinion regarding the merits of shelter versus residential houses and it brought attention to the concept of shelter-type people. Such conflicts will probably surface again as the Community strives towards the legitimate goal of making the house quieter and more peaceful . . .
>
> We have a few, very few, people who are not enough together to modify their conduct. The far greater majority *are* able to change and able to appreciate peace and co-operation. To deny that is to make morons of them, to treat them as drunken teddybears who can be 'great gas' now and again but generally impossible to live with.
>
> Without some order and structure, Simon will have to start from scratch every six months and will have to justify and explain everything that has been done over the past ten years, because every individual in the organisation has the right of private interpretation of the Simon principles. The Executive Committee must plan policy and must be able to implement it.
>
> (*Annual General Report*, 1979)

In the course of 1979, it was decided to appoint a Project Leader for the existing house in Seán McDermott Street; Brendan McCarry took up the post and stayed for six months. Subsequently Teresa Connolly-Mukerjee was appointed to the post, which she held from April 1980 until July 1982. When she began her period of employment with Simon she was responsible for one house (36) and ten residents. But plans were afoot to develop this project, along carefully defined lines. At the 1980 Annual General Meeting the chairman found himself yet again explaining the policy of the Seán McDermott Street project and the reasons behind that policy.

> So let us first look back at the development of the project over the last few years. It is five years since John Long, as Social Worker, employed by the Community, first pointed out that we had no place for our older people. Gradually the Committee shared John's concern and gradually, through 1978, we began to look to No. 36 Seán McDermott Street, as the house for such a project. At the planning meeting in January of last year, the idea was taken a step further when we decided that No. 36 Seán McDermott Street would be a house for 'enfeebled people', i.e., people who are not necessarily very old, but who are not able for, or who simply want to get away from, the daily trudge on the streets and nights in the Shelter.
>
> By April of last year we knew that the second house in Seán McDermott Street was coming our way and we then became more specific in our plans. It was agreed that –
>
> 1. both houses are for enfeebled people;
> 2. the maximum number of residents in each house would be twelve;
> 3. they would be separate projects in separate houses – the quieter people in No. 35;
> 4. the object of the houses is –
>   (a) to care for people and
>   (b) to aim at community living by encouraging participation by all residents in the running of the houses;
> 5. residents should be selected for the houses by a joint meeting of the Management Committees of Seán McDermott Street and the Shelter. In choosing the residents, these broad guidelines should be as follows:

(a) who needs the houses most?
(b) who can the house cope with?
(c) who is likely to get most advantages from living in the house?

6. before admission new residents should be aware of the conditions and limitations of the houses and should agree to live there.

(*Annual General Report*, 1980)

It was under Teresa Connolly-Mukerjee as Project Leader, that official Simon policy began to be implemented in 36; and it was she, also, who supervised the beginnings of 35 as a residential house. An Irish woman married to an Indian, she had spent some years working among the poor in India. She was, in her late forties, older than most Simon employees; she had great organisational abilities. As in the Shelter, the position of Project Leader was one of crucial importance. Teresa was responsible for supervising and co-ordinating the efforts of the full-time worker team. She was also expected to take an individual interest in the residents, ensuring that they were comfortable, happy and in reasonable health. If some of them wished to move on from Simon, she assisted them in their search for alternative housing, and ensured that they were visited on a regular basis. Co-workers who came to the house also relied on her for guidance. She did not, however, take the place of the House Management Committee, but rather encouraged such a committee to meet regularly. She was concerned that resident representatives from each house would take their places on the Management Committee; this meant that residents did genuinely have a say in the running of their house.

In May 1981 the four men from the Fairview house gathered together their personal belongings and moved back to the city centre, to 35 Seán McDermott Street. Situated beside the parish church, this was a large three-storey house with a basement, and when the restructuring work was completed, it became a kind of multipurpose house, reminiscent of 42 Harcourt Street. One large room in the basement became the headquarters for the soup-run, and another part of the basement was the site of the new laundry. The main section of the house consisted of living and sleeping areas for the complement of twelve residents who would eventually live there. Next door, in a smaller house, which also comprised three storeys and a basement, lived the senior citizens of Dublin Simon. In 1981 the average age of the residents there was fifty-nine – and three members of the Community were about to celebrate their eightieth birthdays.

By August 1981 the laundry had begun to function. Automatic washers and a tumble dryer had been bought with part of the Work Project grant. A couple of the men were immediately interested in the work, which consisted, for the most part, in washing blankets and sheets. In the winter of 1982, when I visited the laundry, the average monthly intake was three hundred and eighty blankets and four bags of sheets from the Shelter, thirty blankets and two bags of sheets from the two houses, and thirty blankets from Exchange House (a centre for Travellers) who were paying 60p a blanket. I met the two men, both residents, who were working there. Neither of them proved very talkative, but I sensed that they had a professional approach to their work. All around the spacious laundry were piles of clean, neatly folded blankets. I later discovered that the saving to Simon by doing its laundry in this manner, was in the region of £200 a month.

Meanwhile, upstairs in 35, a new Community had begun to form. The men from Fairview had moved in first; after a few months other residents, who had been living in the Shelter, joined them, and full-time workers were recruited for the house. Some co-workers who had been friendly with individual residents, either in the Shelter or in Fairview, now showed their loyalty by dropping in to visit their friends. But in April 1982 disaster struck in Seán McDermott Street. A fire broke out in one of the top-floor bedrooms in 36. Fortunately none of the residents were injured, but the house was rendered uninhabitable. So the residents moved into the newly established Community in 35. The large first-floor conference room which had been designed for meetings and parties was converted temporarily into a dormitory. With minor rearrangements 35 proved able to cope with all twenty-two residents. This situation lasted for a year.

Carmel Bradley was aware of a scheme whereby prisoners in Mountjoy did renovation work for some charities. After cutting through a great deal of red tape, she managed to get permission for the prisoners to work on 36. They worked with enthusiasm under the supervision of their warders. Unfortunately, later that year, the prison officers went on a go-slow and the work had to be halted. Eventually the prisoners did return and by April 1983 they had the house in splendid condition once again. This incident showed the extent to which Dublin Simon had progressed over the years. Such an occurrence could have led to a crisis situation; instead the Project Leader, workers and residents were able to ensure that day-to-day life could proceed with a minimum of discomfort.

I visited 35 Seán McDermott Street while renovation work was in progress next door. The house was so spacious that I was not immediately aware of any overcrowding. To the right as I entered was a large sitting-room equipped with colour television, two couches and some easy chairs; with a big fire, it was a comfortable, homely room. In one corner there was a bed; Sadie, an invalid from 36 slept there at night. She seemed to spend much of the day in her wheelchair, facing the window. The ground floor windows of the house are protected by wire meshing, otherwise there would be danger of the local youngsters breaking in. The residents use this room a good deal to relax in; the television is nearly always on.

To the left of the hallway was a dining room with a door leading into the kitchen. Meals were served there at specific times. There was a radio in this room which provided an alternative for those who did not wish to watch television. In the evenings there were often card games or draughts in progress, and other residents enjoyed the newspapers. Although there was central heating in the house, the dining room had a fireplace and in cold weather the fire added that special atmosphere to the room. The kitchen was often a hive of activity, what with cooking meals for between twenty and thirty people, baking bread, and making frequent cups of tea. An air of hospitality pervaded the house, and there was a great welcome for co-workers as they arrived. Relationships between the workers and residents seemed easygoing. But at times there was tension, when people were bored, had no money for a drink, or were feeling peeved with each other.

Sunday morning was one such occasion. The dining room

was cosy, with a good fire going, and the smell of roast pork assailed my nostrils as the kitchen door opened. Chrissie, one of the workers, was putting a massive pot of potatoes on to boil, while one of the residents prepared a tray of them for roasting. Another worker poured on steaming custard as the last addition to the Sunday trifle. But despite all this, the atmosphere in the dining room was heavy. The Sunday papers were scattered around. A couple of men had sore heads from the night before; others were perhaps, however involuntarily, recalling the Sundays of other times. One resident said that he had liked to have sex with his wife on a Sunday afternoon! Others were wondering if I would take them for a drive to the Park – it would just be something different.

'Do you find Sunday pleasant?' I asked one man.

'No, it's the worst day of all. Everywhere is closed. It's depressing even to take a walk around.'

The house was comfortable, the residents would have a good dinner and were free to decide how to spend the rest of the day. Nevertheless, the dominant air was one of dissatisfaction and lethargy.

There were four full-time workers in Seán McDermott Street during this period – two male, two female – and Brigid Webber was the Project Leader. She had replaced Teresa, who left in July 1982. Brigid had done full-time work in the Shelter before coming to the residential houses. She was a quiet woman in her twenties with a welcoming manner. She showed me around the house one afternoon. The bedrooms were tidy and airy – roughly four residents to a room. There was a workers' bedroom also. The early Simon custom of workers and residents sharing sleeping accommodation no longer obtained. Toilet and shower facilities were more than adequate. Brigid showed me the garden of 35 with great pride. It had been just a pile of rubble when the house opened. In less than a year, one of the residents had converted it into a thriving garden producing plenty of fresh vegetables. I began to understand why Carmel Bradley had seen the establishment of the Seán McDermott Street houses as one of the high points in the history of Dublin Simon.

The new Shelter

Many of the people I spoke to were critical of the physical conditions in the Dublin Simon Night Shelter. Former workers raised their eyes to heaven. Committee members shook their heads sadly. The residents themselves cursed with vehemence, particularly about the quality of the plumbing. After my own visit, I found myself echoing the words of Gerry Fulham in the 1982 *Annual General Report*:

> Despite continuing maintenance, the Shelter is in appalling physical condition which serves to highlight the pressing need for a new Shelter. It is my earnest hope that by the time the next A.G.M. comes around, those whom we are now caring for in 9/10 Sarsfield Quay will be living in much better surroundings.

Unfortunately, Gerry's 'earnest hope' was not realised. The 1983 Annual General Meeting did come around, and the Shelter was still on the Quay.

In 1976, a major renovation job had taken place in the Sarsfield Quay houses. Justin O'Brien had encouraged Community members to look on the houses as a 'brand new Shelter'. But no amount of positive thinking could alter the reality; 9 & 10 Sarsfield Quay were not structurally suitable as a Night Shelter. In 1977, a further renovation job was carried out; yet the 1978 *Annual General Report* says:

> The structure itself remains most unsatisfactory because it is uncleanable and it is a constant fire hazard. But the exciting news is that two Principal Officers of the Corporation gave us positive hope of a new purpose-built Shelter in the not-too-distant future.

I suppose that the phrase 'the not-too-distant future' can be measured in years, in decades, or in centuries according to one's point of view! Whatever the system of measurement, the Dublin Simon Community still did not have, by the end of 1984, 'a new purpose-built Shelter'. The 1979 *Annual General Report* makes little comment on the topic; that was the year that Seán McDermott Street policy seemed to dominate Community discussion. But once again in 1980 the notion of the new Shelter raised its timid head. Politicians, including the then Taoiseach, Mr Charles Haughey, Corporation officials, and various religious orders were all approached. A co-worker chose the design of a new Shelter as the subject matter for his architectural thesis. Some donations came from the religious orders, and Jim Roche got second class honours for his thesis, but Dublin Simon failed to get the much coveted new Shelter.

1981 saw little progress in this direction, but the following year a major decision was made. The Executive realised that as there was little likelihood of getting a place free of charge they were faced with two options. They could try to buy an existing building which might be suitable, or they could negotiate with the Corporation for a vacant site and build a Shelter to their own design. Either option was going to be extremely expensive. Financial advisors mentioned the figure of £300,000. Dublin Simon did not have that kind of money. Already their annual expenditure was soaring; in the 1982 financial year they had spent £124,106, while their income had only amounted to £118,047. Nevertheless, the search continued and in July 1982 a building in a suitable location came up for sale. Situated on Usher's Island, it was a massive five-storey warehouse, owned by Drummonds, the seed merchants. Having visited it, members of the Executive were of the opinion that, despite some drawbacks, the building had great potential, and an auctioneer had suggested that it could be bought for £150,000.

The Simon Executive decided to attempt to buy the warehouse. In the hope of getting financial aid they prepared a submission for the Eastern Health Board. In October 1982 they got word that the Health Board had allocated £150,000 (of EC Social Fund money) to help Simon provide a new Night Shelter. It looked as though the tide had turned for Dublin Simon. In fact, terrible frustration was to follow.

Once the Committee had decided to attempt to purchase Drummonds they appointed a sub-committee to act on their behalf – Josephine Mitchell, Frank Maguire, Joe Reynolds, Paddy Stronge and Frank O'Leary. Auctioneer James Kinahan made a bid on their behalf; he agreed with the vendor on a price of £160,000. The owners wanted the deal closed by February 1983, which left Dublin Simon under considerable pressure as they had to negotiate planning permission and have the title deeds examined. Both of these tasks gave rise to difficulties. Regarding the planning permission, it transpired that Usher's Quay was earmarked for road-widening. This meant that fourteen feet would have to be cut off the front of the building, thus rendering it virtually useless to Simon. After lengthy discussion and argument, Dublin Corporation officials verbally agreed as a gesture of goodwill,

> that Simon should buy the site; that the Corporation would buy from Simon and then proceed to demolish, to take off the 14 feet for road widening and donate the vacant site to Simon.
>
> (*Annual General Report*, 1983)

It would then be possible for Simon to build their own Shelter. The title deeds, however, proved very comlex. For legal reasons, negotiations towards sale had to take place through a receiver. Meanwhile the property had been badly vandalised. But this, it seemed, would make little difference to the agreed price of the site. So, by October 1983, the chairman had to report once again to the Annual General Meeting that Dublin Simon was simply 'getting closer' to the provision of a new Shelter.

Despite the difficult circumstances, those working in the Shelter continued to give of their care and good humour. In the course of 1983, the House Management Committee, under the chairmanship of Gerry Dee, was active and effective. Residents' meetings were held frequently and resulted in a good community atmosphere. A number of the residents were referred from the Shelter to Seán McDermott Street. Nevertheless, there were up to sixty people on the Quay each night. Co-workers and full-time workers did their best under Gerry Fulham's supervision, to cope with the leaks and the flooding and the blocked sewers.

When Dublin Simon had originally decided on a purpose-built Night Shelter they had envisaged a building which could cater for seventy people. As negotiations over the purchase of the site dragged on, however, Community members began to question the wisdom of such a plan. They decided to research the matter and in February 1985, a team of five – including Tommy, a long-term Simon resident and Gerry Fulham, Project Manager of the Shelter – looked at a variety of Shelter type accommodation in the Greater London area. The general consensus among this team was that a much smaller Shelter – approximately thirty beds – should be built on the Usher's Island site. Such a Shelter would cater specifically for short-term emergency accommodation.

In February 1985 the Usher's Island site was finally bought by Dublin Simon. By June, what remained of the building had been demolished. And in November 1985 Dublin Simon was granted full planning permission for a thirty bed Shelter with the option of building two smaller houses on the site, if they so wished. Mr Pat Claffey, 1985/86 Chairman of the Dublin Community, told me that the Work Project would also operate from the Usher's Island site, as would the soup-run. There were plans, too, for a second-hand furniture shop.

Meanwhile, 1985 proved a decisive year for the old Shelter on the Quays. On 8 February the Dangerous Buildings Section of Dublin Corporation gave the Simon Community fourteen days to vacate their Sarsfield Quay premises. This came as something of a shock for while the Community had often highlighted the fact that conditions in the Shelter were far from perfect, they did not expect to be asked to move on at such short notice. The Housing Department of the Corporation, however, offered them the old Fire Station in Buckingham Street which had been vacated six months previously. Although initially Simon were loathe to accept this offer because of their two residential houses close by in Seán McDermott Street, they really had no option.

On 4 March 1985 the Dublin Simon Community vacated the premises at Sarsfield Quay which had been 'home' for some residents since 1971. By all accounts the move to Buckingham Street Fire Station was managed smoothly and both residents and workers settled into their new quarters, where they remained for four years under the calm and competent leadership of Gerry Fulham.

Meanwhile in June 1988 the foundation stone of the Usher's Island Shelter was laid. A year later the purpose-built Simon complex – comprising a thirty bed Night Shelter, a residential house for eleven former Shelter residents, a soup kitchen and premises for a Work Project – was completed. Dublin Simon moved from Buckingham Street in June 1989, and the Shelter was officially opened by President Hillery the following September. By then Gerry Fulham had resigned from his post as

Project Leader – a position he had held for nine years. This constitutes a record in the history of Simon staffing. Gerry's contribution to the Community was incalculable, his presence having had a stabilising influence on life in the Shelter throughout the eighties.

From the outset the new Shelter was geared towards short-term emergency accommodation with an emphasis on effective referral. At this stage in its development Dublin Simon was keen to define the limits of the service it could provide. With this in mind a worker, whose brief was to research and monitor referral of residents from the Shelter, was employed in 1990.

8

CARING AND CAMPAIGNING

Signs of the times

The Simon Community in Ireland has not existed in a social or political vacuum. Since its tentative beginnings in Dublin in 1969 it has grown and developed organisationally against the backdrop of Irish society, which has itself undergone major changes during this period. In the early seventies Ireland was still basking in the glorious sunshine of apparently unlimited economic growth. There were ample job opportunities. There did not appear to be any critical shortage of public funds. Dublin Simon, in those early days, received a large proportion of its income in the form of donations, many of which were anonymous. Young people could afford to 'drop out' for a while in order to become full-time workers, without putting their career opportunities at risk. In fact some of the early full-time workers have since held positions of national importance. John Long was employed as special advisor to Ruairi Quinn TD during his term as Minister for Labour. Jim Murray became Ireland's first Director of Consumer Affairs.

By the mid-seventies Ireland had been hit by the recession caused by the 1973 oil crisis. The future no longer appeared so hopeful. There was the prospect of cuts in public spending. The points system for university entry was becoming ever more complex and second-level students were warned that only the winners in the education competition would have a chance of secure, well-paid employment. Meanwhile there was a greater concentration of the population in urban areas, and unemployment figures were on the increase. The crime rate began to rise and the ordinary citizen became acutely concerned about issues of law and order. Sympathy towards the deprived, on the one hand, tended to be accompanied, on the other, by a harsh attitude towards 'wrongdoers'. This attitude was very much to the fore during 1977 when the issue of Loughan House, sometimes referred to as 'The Children's Prison', was publicly debated.

It was during this period that Dublin Simon encountered such opposition in Chapelizod and Fairview. Among the criticisms levelled at Simon by Residents' Associations was that their areas would get a bad name. As a result their property would be devalued. House owners could hardly be blamed for their concern; many of them were overburdened with large mortgages.

With the onset of the eighties, the now proverbial 'gloom and doom' atmosphere became more pervasive. The problem of unemployment was reaching crisis proportions. Factories began to close down, and there were cutbacks even in the public sector. The Irish people showed their dissatisfaction with the performance of their politicians when they went to the ballot boxes. There were three changes of government in the space of eighteen months. Still things grew worse. Factory closures became daily announcements. Less and less money was being made available in grant form to cultural and charitable organisations. Meanwhile maintenance costs soared; the cost of food, petrol, electricity and postage stamps made them seem like luxury items. The disposable income of the ordinary citizen grew smaller. Dublin Simon found that donations were harder to get.

Since 1976, the Committee had been in the habit of holding an annual planning meeting after each Annual General Meeting. Budgeting was a feature of this exercise. Paddy Stronge, an accountant who offered his services in a voluntary capacity, acted as an adviser on financial affairs. Simon's basic aim was to stay in the black, to ensure that their expenditure did not exceed their income. Until 1982 they managed to achieve their objective. By the 1983 Annual General Meeting they were genuinely concerned about finance.

> Finance was a big source of worry during the last year. In November we were £16,000 in the red. By mid-December that had increased to £17,000. A better than usual inflow at Christmas – £24,000 – cleared those debts but by April of this year we needed £10,000 to pay off some debts. Granted, quite a lot of our expenditure at that time was

> for capital purposes – the renovation of the Melrose Avenue And Seán Mac [*sic*] (No. 36) houses. But almost every year there is some big renovation job to be done. Gathering in the funds is becoming more difficult as the recession goes on. We must economise where possible.

This question of economy was to become a central issue. The main solution proposed at the 1983 Annual General Meeting was similar to the solutions being put forward by many of the commercial enterprises in the country:

> Arising out of the points raised here last year and previous years regarding our expenditure on salaries . . . the Executive Committee set out to examine how and where we could increase voluntary input in our Community. The only area where this seemed possible was in our office where we felt we could re-organise our structure and reduce the number of paid staff by making more use of voluntary help. The future office we began to visualise would be run by an office supervisor/manager and perhaps a telephonist/typist with voluntary help where required. We envisage the book-keeping being done by a retired accountant or book-keeper on a part-time and hopefully on a voluntary basis. We also envisage three new sub-committees: one for Finance (chaired by a Treasurer who would be a member of Executive), one for Education and one for Maintenance.
>
> To achieve these aims, it would be necessary to make our present office staff redundant. After long and careful consideration of all aspects of our proposal, we put it, as a proposal, to the Administration staff on 31st August last. Since then we had some discussions with the staff and their Union representative. Talks are still in progress.
>
> (*Annual General Report*, 1983)

This information led to a lengthy discussion at the 1983 Annual General Meeting, which was reported in *Link* (October 1983):

> Several people said that it was the wrong decision, that volunteers in Administration were a bad idea, . . . and that it could have waited and been put forward as a proposal to the A.G.M. There was disagreement on how it was presented to the staff with the Executive saying it was presented as a

proposal and speakers from the floor claiming that it was more like a decision. Cathy Power [herself a staff member] talked of the Staffs' attitudes to the redundancies. She said they didn't think it would work and that politically it was a bad decision for Simon. She also tried to enlarge the debate to discuss the powers of the Executive and Simon's attitude to paid staff. Jack Ryan [a co-worker of long standing] made a proposal that 'the Executive Committee's decision to make the office staff redundant should not be implemented'. The proposal was later changed to 'This A.G.M. strongly recommends that the office staff redundancies should not be implemented'. Jack went on to talk of why he was opposed to the redundancies. He said that as a trade unionist he did not agree with redundancies. He talked of the difficulty of working under a committee when one year they decide something and next year a different committee decide something else. Jack also said that if we were paying staff too much, it was we who made this mistake and why should they take the blame for our mistakes.

Bobby Eager said that when he went forward for election to the Executive he thought they were there to run the Community. He spoke of a lack of trust in the Executive and said that if you don't agree with Executive's decisions, you change them at the A.G.M. . . .

Frank O'Leary thanked those who stood up and said they had previously complained about expenditure on salaries. He said that Executive felt that they were reflecting a genuine 'grass-root' feeling. Jack Ryan's second proposal was put to the meeting and was passed by forty seven votes to twenty one with ten abstentions. These abstentions included office staff who felt the problem was no longer theirs but one for Dublin Simon.

This debate gave rise to considerable confusion and bad feeling. Carmel Bradley, Cathy Power and Evelyn Bracken were eventually made redundant. The incident raises a number of crucial questions in relation to voluntary organisations and their relationship with their salaried staff. The National Social Service Board in its discussion document, *The Development of Voluntary Social Services in Ireland* (Dublin, 1982), makes the following comment:

Voluntary bodies employing full-time paid staff face many problems related to working conditions and terms of employment. In areas such as remuneration, superannuation and holidays they often find it difficult to offer terms which can match those offered by statutory agencies (and here must be included the non-statutory welfare agencies). For these reasons voluntary bodies sometimes find it hard to recruit the right kind of staff or there may be problems with high turnover of staff. From an employee point of view voluntary bodies sometimes make bad employers since they may be tempted to treat employees as paid volunteers rather than employees.

Cathy Power, in an article entitled 'Paid Workers in Simon', written during her period of employment, seems to bear out this point from her own experience.

> It is a privilege to work in an organisation to which you are committed, but it is also a strain in many ways. One is expected not only to be a good employee, but also a good volunteer, and it is hard for those who are giving their time for nothing not to expect much more from the employees within the Community than they themselves are willing to give to their own employers. Maybe I was a particularly bad employee in the past, but it makes me smile to think of the difference in my attitude to my job now compared to what it was like in the other places in which I worked, where, for example, overtime payment was taken for granted, where you chose to take your holidays when it suited you, not having to take into account that the A.G.M. was coming up, or that the end of the financial year was looming on the horizon and that you could not be spared, where you left the office at the end of the day and forgot about it. What I'm doing now is no big deal, I'm not looking for particular praise for it. It is only what I would expect from any Simon employee, but I am *not* a volunteer and until my formal employment with Simon ends, I don't intend to become one.
>
> (*Simon Ireland Newsletter*, April 1982)

When a voluntary organisation decides to employ staff, it is taking a serious step. Being a good employer is not an easy task. It involves skills and expertise other than those necessary in an organisation made up entirely of volunteers. In this country, until recently, certain workers who were held in high esteem by the general public were nevertheless poorly paid. The nursing profession is a case in point. Yet when nurses began to demand a realistic salary many people were scandalised. Nursing, after all, was a vocation. Such mercenary considerations as wage increases were just not appropriate for those who had a vocation to care for the sick.

This kind of thinking does not allow for two basic facts of life in our western, capitalist economy. Firstly, not even the most spiritual among us can afford to live on fresh air. Housing, food, transport – even those with a 'vocation' must pay for these. Secondly, whether we like it or not, money is a major symbol of esteem in our society. He or she who does a good job deserves to be paid for it in the currency which is valued – money. That is what increments and career structures are all about. So if a voluntary organisation decided to employ staff – on a long-term, professional basis – it is vital that such staff should not end up feeling guilty about the salaries they receive, simply because they are working for a 'caring' organisation. In times of recession this is particularly important.

The Dublin Simon office was managed for six months by two co-workers, who were employed in a temporary, full-time capacity. Meanwhile the Executive Committee decided to advertise for an Office Manager. They hoped to recruit someone with previous experience in social work. He or she was to be the only full-time administrative employee. The role of Office Manager differed from that of Administrator in two ways. The Manager would not have authority over other staff, nor would he have responsibility for finance. In February 1984 the post was filled. A rota of volunteers was drawn up in order to deal with the secretarial side of Dublin Simon work.

'They're my friends'

You may have often wondered who works for Simon – who are the volunteers, where do they come from, how long do they stay? Already, in the course of the story of Dublin Simon, you have met some of them – women and men, young and, dare I say, middle-aged. They have come in their hundreds to offer their services to the Community. Some stay only for a short period, for others Simon becomes part of their lives. These volunteers often socialise together, they form deep friendships, and sometimes they marry each other. There have been many Simon weddings over the years, most of them performed by Frank O'Leary in his capacity as Franciscan priest. Indeed it may not be too long now until there will be a second generation of Simon workers; there have been many christenings.

Initially Simon attracted people because it was a new and unconventional organisation. And homelessness was a 'new' and startling social issue. Those who offered their services did so either as full-time or part-time workers. The latter became known as co-workers. Full-timers worked in the Shelter or in the residential houses and were recruited through the National Office. They stayed anything from three months to a year. They were not encouraged to spend longer than a year in the houses; full-time work, because of the intensity involved, was necessarily a short-term commitment. Some of them became co-workers after their full-time stint, and some served as Committee members.

There was no shortage of full-timers at the beginning, and many of them stayed for up to a year. At that time people tended to see Simon as an alternative way of life. Dick Shannon, no doubt remembering his own humble origins in Dublin Simon, wrote about that period in the *Simon Ireland Newsletter* of September 1977:

> At the beginning it was easy enough to attract committed and enthusiastic people to Simon which was then a new, fresh and unconventional movement attempting to provide a radical (in the true sense of that word) alternative to caring for people. It was a time when there was no shortage of people dissatisfied with the status quo; when there was an abundance of visionaries, revolutionaries and radicals; when students and young people generally felt secure in not conforming and in doing their own thing; when it was fashionable for people to experiment in living like the birds of the air and the lilies of the field in communes in Dalkey or Dingle.

Dick wrote at a time when recruitment was going through a difficult phase. He was conscious that times had changed, and so had attitudes and values. He was not the only person to notice these changes. Bob Cashman, having resigned from the Executive Committee in 1974, returned by popular demand in 1976. In a letter written in August 1977 to Ian Hart, he comments on the situation:

> Since my return to the Committee in 1976, I have been fascinated by the change in the full-time workers. There seems to be far less 'hassle', far less villainy and far less vitality than in the early seventies. Whether this is a result of the assessments, changing times, or the poachers turned gamekeepers on the Committee is not yet clear to me. Perhaps the quest for balance and sanity has gone too far.

In the mid-seventies there did not appear to be any great clarity within Dublin Simon about the role of the full-time volunteer. New groups of workers came to the projects and very often they did not know what was expected of them. They found themselves in a vacuum, and when they were unable to implement policy, in the Shelter for example, they brought their problems to Executive level. They were looking for both guidance and affirmation. The Executive Committee felt that the problems of the local projects should be dealt with by the workers in conjunction with the House Management Committees. But this did not seem to work. There was a disturbingly high turnover of full-time workers. Gradually the Executive Committee became clearer about what was happening. The old tradition of the full-time workers who had a strong hand in shaping policy and therefore a strong sense of their own role within the Community, had died. With it, perhaps, had died some of the 'vitality' of which Bob Cashman spoke. The role of the full-time volunteer within Dublin Simon had to be re-examined and re-defined. Jim Murray, who was vice-chairman in 1977, had some suggestions to make in this regard:

> For all its faults, the function of the Simon Executive is to provide (and if necessary impose) consistency but this is not possible with such a high turnover of workers. . . .
>
> The way to keep workers lies in limiting the numbers we

are trying to help, in proper induction procedures after acceptance, in giving new workers defined and concrete duties under supervision, and in making it clear that 'caring' requires discipline and an unrelenting commitment to doing ordinary day-to-day practical things. To achieve all this, it might be necessary to employ a full-time paid, professional supervisor for each project.

(*Simon Ireland Newsletter*, October 1977)

As soon as Dublin Simon employed Project Leaders, the situation began to improve. Meanwhile the National Office had begun to pay more attention to training sessions for volunteers. In 1978 the first National Simon Conference was held. In the course of a residential weekend in comfortable surroundings, full-time workers and co-workers from different Communities had a chance to chat informally and to benefit from formal addresses on relevant topics. The National Conference has since become an annual event. The 1984 Conference had sessions on Homelessness – The Solution? (the speaker was David Donnison of Glasgow Council for the Single Homeless), on Caring and the Christian (the speaker was Frank O'Leary) and workshops on Travellers (Nan Joyce, Mervyn Ennis), Housing Options for the Homeless (Bernard Thompson), and Welfare and the Homeless (John Brophy).

Over the last few years, workshops, specifically for full-time workers, have also been held. Topics have included the role of the full-time worker, aggression and the door, mental illness, and burnout.* Since 1980 the full-time worker situation has stabilised. Volunteers have been staying longer; in Dublin the average length of stay in 1983 was eight months. Of the thirty-one full-time workers who served in the course of that year, eighteen were male and thirteen were female. All but one were under the age of thirty. Talking to some of these workers I got the impression that they had a clear idea of what they were about. The existence of the Project Leaders seemed to help them a great deal. The full-time workers may well differ from those in the early days, but then they function within an organisation which is, in structural terms at least, quite different from the early Community on the Quay.

---

*A recently-coined term describing the exhaustion social workers can suffer due to the intensity of their work.

There has, from time to time, been criticism of the whole notion of short-term volunteers. A crucial part of the full-time worker's contribution is his or her ability and willingness to relate to the residents. Friendship is a central part of the Simon service. Is it good, then, people wonder, that workers should come, stay for a few months, build up a relationship with some of the residents, and then disappear? On the surface the answer would seem to be no. Dick Shannon, however, pointed out to me that many of the ordinary relationships in our lives are of a transitory nature. We study or work somewhere for a year or two; we become friends with our colleagues; and then we move on. Usually we make new friends, but we do not forget the old ones. Where the bonds have been deep, we keep in touch – by phone, by letter, and of course the occasional visit. This is what often happens in Simon. Full-time workers leave and are replaced; but often they write to the residents or drop in on a social visit when in town. Many foreigners have worked in Simon. They, too, keep in touch. I know of one Dutch woman who writes quite regularly to a couple of the residents. She looks forward very much to visiting Simon each time she returns to Ireland.

But, as you say, we also need stable relationships in our lives. We need to know that not everyone will move on. What can the volunteer provide for the Simon resident at this level? It is in response to this kind of question that we need to look at the role of the co-worker, and particularly the long-term co-worker, in Dublin Simon. For many years co-workers were, I suspect, looked on as second-class citizens in Simon. After all, they did not give up their jobs. they only came down one night a week; they continued to live in their comfortable homes. Yet in many senses it is the co-workers who have provided the real continuity for the residents in Dublin Simon. I was particularly struck by this fact when I talked with Tommy, a long-term resident, who ended up in hospital for a few days as a result of a blackout. He had been lonely and without cigarettes until he had managed to get the hospital administration to inform the Simon Shelter of his whereabouts. Within twenty four hours, two co-workers were in to see him; having come straight from work, they had sat on the hospital steps for half an hour until visiting time began. I asked Tommy how he felt about the long-term co-workers – mentioning Fidelma Bonass, Rita Fagan, Geraldine Regan – and he said, 'Well they're my friends, aren't they?'

Co-workers are completely responsible for a number of Simon projects. The soup-run, that important initial contact with those sleeping rough, has been co-ordinated by them all through the years. In 1983 they continued to meet a relatively stable group of about twenty people every night – within a three-mile radius of the city centre. Subsequently, they returned to the idea – old in Simon terms – that of providing an open-air soup kitchen, nightly, in the Smithfield area. In a report of 24 June 1984, Dublin Simon noted that:

> Our mobile soup kitchen at Arran Quay is booming, with up to thirty people availing of the tea, soup and sandwiches each night. Many of them are young.

Closely linked with the soup-run is the project known as follow-up. This, too, is a co-worker venture. Co-ordinated by Pat Normanly, it ensures that Simon residents or soup-run contacts are visited while in hospital or in prison. Many follow-up workers have been with Simon many years; some like Pat Normanly have done a stint of full-time work and have been co-workers on various other projects. In her thirties, Pat is of medium build and has short, red hair. Originally from Co. Sligo, she has been in Dublin all her working life, where she is employed by CIE. Since she has tended to socialise mainly within Simon circles, it did not come as such a great surprise when she married another Simon worker of long standing. The man concerned, Pat Claffey, is a former chairman of the Executive Committee. Bearded and bespectacled, Pat is a man of strong views. He, too, has a full-time worker background and his ordinary job is in residential childcare. The Community as a whole, both residents and workers, were delighted about this match.

Co-workers have always been recruited directly through the Dublin Simon office. A system of introductory meetings has been a part of their initiation. But while there has always been a steady nucleus of co-workers, the old reliables, there have been many occasions when there have not been enough active part-time volunteers in the Community. Some projects tend to attract people – the soup-run and the Shelter. But all too often the residential houses miss out. Co-workers were thin on the ground in Harcourt Street and in Fairview, and now the same complaint is heard from the houses in Seán McDermott Street. And the high turnover of co-workers has given cause for concern over the years. The 1982 *Annual General Report* bears witness to this. 'I believe,' the Chairman said,

> we should *never* have an acute shortage of co-workers. I believe we have a huge harvest of young people who want to work with Simon. I believe that the loss/turnover in co-worker ranks is far too high. I think that because potential volunteers are so numerous we are inclined to regard them as expendable when every good member should be seen as a precious possession. It should not be necessary for any-one to go round the pubs on a Saturday night looking for someone to help at the soup-run. Conclusion: we still have not found the right formula/system/person for introducing, training, motivating and holding a much larger percentage of our co-workers.

The following year Cathy Power gave an account in the *Annual General Report* of how the approach to recruitment and initiation had developed:

> The introductory sessions now take place every three months in the new format. This involves candidates com-pleting application forms and attending a one-day intro-ductory which includes talks on the philosophy of Simon, case histories, role play and group discussion. I feel that this approach has been more effective in keeping co-workers and also is of benefit to those long-term co-workers who participate as group leaders for the day. About fifty per cent of those who attend the first public meeting, with the intention of joining Simon, do not eventually attend the full-day introductory. This in itself is a measure of the success of the new system as it means that either these people were not interested enough to complete the form and return it, or that on attempting to complete the form

they themselves realised that they were not suited to working in the Community.

Co-workers will always be needed in Dublin Simon; without them the Community cannot survive. An organisation like Simon needs people with a variety of talents. Those of a literary bent might wish to help with *Link*, the internal newsletter. Financial whizz kids are desperately needed, to raise the money. People who would describe themselves as 'good company' might have a lot to offer by spending one evening a week in Seán McDermott Street, getting to know some of the residents. And of course volunteers with good health and plenty of energy will always be needed on the soup-run and in the Shelter.

Street workers – a new development

The concept of 'taking the initiative', going out to find people in need rather than waiting for them to come, has been a distinctive feature of the Simon Community right from the beginning. Dublin Simon has taken the initiative in many ways over the years – the soup-run, follow-up work, survey work. In September 1984 they decided to put a new project of this kind into action on a trial basis. With the help of the Youth Employment Agency/Teamwork Scheme they employed two former full-time workers as 'Street Workers'.

Street workers can complement the work already being done by the soup-run. During the day they may meet people around the city that the soup-run has failed to contact. This might involve approaching someone on the street, who appears homeless or disorientated, offering him a cigarette, inviting him for a cup of coffee and a chat. Or a Street Worker may be able to follow up on people with whom the soup-run has already made a basic contact.

Street Work usually involves a great deal of referral. People who find themselves temporarily homeless often need help in order to find accommodation or to make a Social Welfare claim. During the period of the Pilot Project (1984/85), Dublin Simon Street Workers were in contact with a hundred and ten people, the majority of whom were male and in the thirty to fifty age group. The main problems encountered were unemployment, substance abuse, domestic difficulties, psychiatric illness, and Social Welfare problems.

In August 1985 the Dublin Community decided to employ two full-time salaried Street Workers to continue the work which had been initiated by the Y.E.A./Teamwork Pilot Project. Once again they recruited two former full-time workers. As a result of ongoing evaluation it was subsequently decided simply to employ one Outreach Worker who would provide a daytime soup-run where increasing numbers of young people were being discovered.

What real impact are we making?

When Anton Wallich-Clifford decided, in 1963, to make caring and campaigning the twin pillars upon which the Simon Community was to be built, he was something of a prophet. He saw, before many others, the link between the individual homeless person and the structures in our western society which create and perpetuate homelessness as a sociological reality. He wished to care for those who were already homeless, but he also wanted to campaign in order to establish a caring society in which homelessness would no longer exist. Those who cared, he felt, could campaign genuinely because they had first-hand experience of dealing with the victims of a society which was structured in an unjust manner. And in Britain in the sixties the Simon Community was to the fore in the campaign against homelessness.

In Ireland too, the early members of the Community were taken by this idea of campaign. The Simon Community appealed to many people who would not have become involved in other types of caring organisations. Workers talked incessantly about the need for a campaign against homelessness. But there was no consensus about the nature of such a campaign. The crisis over the Northumberland Square houses, in fact, arose against this background. The efforts to integrate Simon residents into suburban areas of Dublin were also prompted by this conviction that Simon must establish a caring society. Dublin Simon Community got its fingers badly burned over the Chapelizod affair, and Committee members began to reconsider how best to influence public opinion in favour of the homeless.

Ian Hart had a particular interest in public education. In the course of the 1970s he appeared frequently on television participating in discussions on homelessness and related issues.

When the question of Loughan House Juvenile Detention Centre was being publicly debated, he spoke out forcefully against it drawing on his own research, with both juvenile delinquents and Simon residents to substantiate his argument. As Chairman of the Management Committee of the Simon house in Fairview, he attended meetings of the Residents' Association in an effort to allay the fears of the local people. He was heartened by the proposal passed at the 1978 National Conference of the Irish Simon Communities, that Simon together with other concerned organisations should present a united front in their effort to combat the causes and consequences of homelessness.

> This move is not before its time. The co-ordinating group should seek to create an all party lobby in the Dáil and in whatever political assembly emerges in Northern Ireland. These lobbies, along with other aims such as the abolition of the Vagrancy Act in the Republic, should press for the development of an overall plan for the homeless . . . .
> (Hart, Ian, *Dublin Simon Community 1971-1976: An Exploration*, ESRI, Dublin 1978, p. 97)

Meanwhile a fiery co-worker with the Cork Simon Community decided that the homeless needed a voice in the political arena. He stood for the Senate election in 1977 as an independent candidate for the National University of Ireland constituency. He did not win a seat. But he gained a surprising number of first preference votes from university graduates to whom he presented himself as a candidate for the poor, and he was not eliminated until the seventeenth count.

Brendan Ryan was elected to Seanad Eireann in 1981, and he has retained his seat in subsequent elections. Strong-willed and fiercely articulate, he has made his voice heard. Brendan is not a politician to be trifled with. A socialist and trade unionist, he believes that the key to effective political action is to press for identifiable and measurable improvements in the way services for the poor and oppressed are administered, and to argue at the same time for longer-term changes in legislation and attitudes. Although he was not taken seriously at first, due to his beard, jeans, and Guevara-style hat, Government ministers learned to listen more carefully as he mobilised one campaign after another, paying great attention to detail. A minister who was unhelpful on a particular issue was likely to find himself in the Senate later that evening defending his policy to an angry senator who knew just how to use the rules and procedure of the Senate to make the Government answerable for its actions.

At the Simon National Conference in 1982, Brendan Ryan, with seven months Senate experience behind him, addressed the gathering on the subject of political challenge. His major concern at the time was the fact that most people who were members of voluntary organisations were not involved in any political (in the broadest sense of that word) activity.

> It is arguable that most people who work in voluntary organisations are unconsciously ensuring that the fundamental structural inequality which produces homelessness, poverty and injustice goes unchallenged . . . .
>
> These are good generous people who devote themselves to voluntary services and who are arguably among the most caring and compassionate group in our society . . . .
>
> But a good question needs to be asked – what real impact are they making? What real change is being achieved? . . . It is one thing to provide a service, important though it be; what have all the combined efforts of all the voluntary organisations done to contribute to a lasting solution to any of the problems they identify and the consequences of which they try to alleviate? That's what we're all doing, we're trying to make up for people's past experiences in one way or another – or their present situation; we're providing a service which alleviates the misery, alleviates the pain. But the question that is well worth asking is – what needs to be done?

At that same conference Bob Cashman also gave a talk in which he reflected on developments within Simon. He prepared for this address, by re-reading the body of Simon literature which had accummulated over the years. Some of his suggestions went a long way towards answering Brendan Ryan's basic question.

> As far as I am concerned, Simon, with all its faults and failings, is great and I am proud of the part I was able to play in its establishment and development. I am satisfied

> that its work in providing shelter, food, support, solace and, in some instances work, is magnificent. But honestly I am not happy about its role and efforts in long-term social issues. . . . The impression which has been on my mind for some time has been reinforced by my rereading – i.e. – that talk and verbosity are substitutes for reflected and considered action. For example, Dick Shannon suggested, as far back as November 1976, a campaign by all organisations to combat prejudice – an educational programme aimed at residents, councillors, legislators, etc., on behalf of the deprived. Has there been any follow up by Simon on this most important issue? . . . In 1978 a decision was reached at the National Conference to set up a coordinating body of voluntary organisations involved in homelessness to examine what action could be taken to press for change. . . . What has Simon done?
>
> The election of Brendan Ryan to the Seanad and the appointment of support staff at the National Office are major events in the political field. I note that Brendan is preparing a Homeless Persons Bill and that this is down for discussion at this conference. Hopefully this matter will get somewhere; then again it may not. But there are other avenues. For example, it has been announced that the Department of the Environment will be issuing a White Paper on housing in the near future. It is open to Simon to approach the Department for discussions on the housing needs of the homeless and to put forward suggestions or proposals for inclusion in the White Paper. However, proposals must be well thought out, costed and put forward in the context of overall housing policy. . . . Should Simon not put forward its views on social planning and social issues to the Government?

By the end of 1984 both Dublin Simon and the National Office had produced results of which even Bob Cashman might have been proud. In March 1982 Brian Harvey was appointed as Information Officer in the National Office. His brief was twofold: as well as assisting Brendan Ryan in the Seanad, he was to initiate research and to prepare solid background information on various aspects of homelessness. Tall and slight in appearance, Brian turned out to have a mind like a computer. By May 1982 a document had been prepared for the Department of the Environment. It was entitled *Housing: An Agenda for Action*, and in it Simon outlined their case for the Department to take responsibility for housing the homeless. Submissions were also prepared that year for the Departments of Health and Finance.

In March 1983 the introduction in the Senate of the *Housing (Homeless Persons) Bill* (see Appendix 3) by Senator Brendan Ryan, made homelessness in Ireland a political issue for the first time. This bill defines a 'homeless person' in law, defines the local authority as responsible for housing him/her and obliges the local authority to provide him/her with public housing. As a result of the Senate debate on this bill, and the publicity it generated, the Simon Community was invited in January 1984 by the Department of the Environment for discussions on government legislation for the homeless. The meeting was a positive one, and the text of the legislation was to be published later in 1984.

However, 1984 passed without the promised text having been published by the Government. In order to highlight the issue Senator Brendan Ryan held a Press conference in May 1985, which was attended by representatives of prominent religious and voluntary organisations. They demanded that the Government pass the 1983 Housing (Homeless Persons) Bill which would have obliged Local Authorities to house the homeless. But it was not until 17 October 1985 that the Minister for the Environment, Mr Liam Kavanagh, announced the publication of the long awaited Government text entitled Housing (Miscellaneous Provisions) Bill, 1985. The delay in publishing the Bill, it emerged, had been due to disagreement among members of the Cabinet about the wording of the clause relating to 'intentionality', a concept which refers specifically to those who have deliberately allowed themselves to become homeless.

It appears that certain Cabinet members, who had themselves been members of Local Authorities, argued forcibly that the clauses referring to people who had made themselves homeless intentionally should be more stringent. As a result, according to the Government Bill, people *who in the Housing Authority's opinion* are deemed to have become homeless deliberately will not qualify for public housing. In Britain a similar clause has been used as a loophole to debar many applicants. And no provision has been made for lodging an appeal.

While Simon Communities throughout Ireland welcomed the main thrust of the proposed legislation they have, nevertheless, severely criticised certain aspects of the Bill. The definition of 'homeless' was found to be too narrow, excluding Travellers, women who cannot gain peaceable entry to their accommodation, and those threatened by homelessness. Concern was also expressed about those clauses relating to 'intentional homelessness' and the concept of 'independent living'. Without certain amendments, therefore, the Simon Communities will not consider the Housing (Miscellaneous Provisions) Bill, 1985 an adequate response to their campaign for a legislative response to the problem of homelessness.

A time lapse of thirteen months occurred between the publication of the Bill and the passing of the second stage in the Dáil. The fact that it had not reached the statute books before the dissolution of the twenty fourth Dáil did not mean that the issue would conveniently disappear. It was now official policy that there was an urgent need for legislation. Voluntary bodies expected it and they intended to make their voices heard.

As a result of an initiative of the Simon National Office a National Campaign for the Homeless was formed in 1984. Over the years various organisations had attempted to meet the needs of specific categories of homeless people. 'Hope', for example, was established in order to work with homeless teenage boys. Both 'Threshold' and 'Centre Care' offer support, information and advice to those experiencing accommodation difficulties. 'St Vincent's Trust' operates as a drop-in day centre for homeless men and women. And in 1984 'Focus Point' was established as a direct outcome of research carried out by Stanislaus Kennedy RSC. It provides a variety of services for those who find themselves homeless in Dublin city.

In 1981 Dublin Simon had decided to form a team of volunteers with the specific aim of discovering how many people in the under-forty age group were sleeping rough in Dublin. Subsequently the survey was extended to include all homeless people who were sleeping rough, with a special section devoted to the under-forties. Because of Ian Hart's involvement with Simon, the Economic and Social Research Institute offered to act in an advisory capacity. The survey was conducted slowly and methodically over a two-year period. In 1983 a report was published in booklet form. This report, unlike so many sociological documents, is highly readable. It includes, together with statistics (see Appendix 2) profiles of homeless people; a description of a typical day in Dublin for one who is homeless; comments on the part that might be played by the Churches and trade unions to combat homelessness; a feature on the homeless and the right to bail; and seven succinct recommendations for immediate action. The report showed that one thousand and forty four hostel beds were used nightly in Dublin, and that ninety-eight people were found sleeping rough. It also pointed to the fact that the number of people under forty, who are genuinely homeless and unable to provide themselves with any accommodation, is increasing.

On the campaigning front, Dublin Simon and the National Office had been working in close alliance. In January 1984 both Frank O'Leary and Brian Harvey delivered addresses to the Housing Committee of Dublin Corporation, in which they outlined the plight of the single homeless in their efforts to get local authority housing. They both stressed that the nature of the points system at that time did not take the reality of homelessness into account.

'The pattern which emerges is as follows,' said Brian Harvey. 'People who sleep rough generally get no points. Those in shelters get, on average, 22-23 points. This is of little use to them. Applicants need about 50 points to get low-demand housing, 65 for middle-demand, and 100-120 for high-demand housing. The system for allocating medical points is clear and satisfactory. The method of allocating "social policy" points is hopelessly confused and unintelligible. It is not adapted to the needs of homeless people. There are no points for being in night shelters and no points for number of years homeless. There are no points for sleeping out, though there *are* for not having cold water on hand.'

'We accept the need for some sort of a points system in the allocation of accommodation,' said Frank O'Leary. 'We propose that points should be given for long-term homelessness – a quota of points per year without a home.

'We further propose that extra points should be given to those who sleep rough because they cannot use the existing hostels.'

Brian Harvey also drew attention to the fact that, while certain categories of homeless people were theoretically entitled to public housing, according to the stated policy of Dublin Corporation, in practice many of them were not even considered. While the Corporation claimed to treat a homeless person over the age of 50 as a senior citizen and thus eligible for accommodation specifically allocated to senior citizens, the following case study, among those cited by Brian Harvey, was but one which showed that this kind of eligibility meant very little.

> Mary R, 69. Dublin night shelter. Old Age Pension. 22 points. Told she is unlikely to get housing and if she does it will be low-demand housing. On the housing list since 1979. Considered likely to get housing sooner as she is female.

Despite the fact that homeless people under fifty *were*, according to the stated policy of Dublin Corporation, considered for public housing where there was a genuine medical or social problem, the Simon Community was advised by the then Housing Manager of the Corporation that families were a priority and that he saw little prospect of the families' waiting list being cleared in the near future, if ever. As a result of the meeting between the Simon Community and Dublin Corporation, the Housing Department decided to allocate fifty flats of medium and high demand at various locations around the city, specifically for the homeless. This variation to the letting priorities was approved by the Department of the Environment in 1984. Such an innovation, while welcome, failed to ensure that stories like the following would not become more common.

> September 4, 1980. The dog pond, Phoenix Park. A man in his 40s, 'tall, strong, full beard, red-flecked, bruised face, hands decomposed', was pulled out. He was known to have slept rough in the area for a long time. Never identified. Did not get, was too young for, public housing.

> September 1980, Eileen K, in her 40s. Died in Camolin, Co. Wexford. Had slept rough for five years in Dublin. Was six stone when admitted to hospital. Did not get, was too young for, public housing.

But where did we go wrong?

When parents discover unpleasant facts about their children's lives, they often ask in a perplexed fashion, 'but where did we go wrong?' For some this is a genuine question; they wish to be as honest as possible about the past and to discover what concrete, remedial measures can be taken in the future. For others it remains a purely rhetorical question. They do not really believe they went wrong at all. Whatever has happened, it is not their fault. So the children themselves must be to blame. In our competitive, consumer-oriented, western society the 'winners' often sound like the parents; and the 'losers' usually act like the children, who for some mysterious reason, have gone astray. In Irish society, the single homeless would certainly be classed among the losers and many Irish citizens would believe that it is their own fault.

There is however, another way of looking at things. A competitive society, by definition, can only work if there are both losers and winners. So the structures of such a society ensure that some will win and others lose. In the past the points system used by the Housing Section of Dublin Corporation did not discriminate sufficiently in favour of the single homeless. As a result of the Housing Act, 1988 however, a new points system is being prepared by the Corporation. Although the single homeless are recognised under the Act, the legislation does not oblige the Local Authority to house them; it simply enables them to do so. Until January 1989 when the Act became operative, it was actually a crime to be homeless in Ireland. Happily the famous clause in the 1824 Vagrancy Act which referred to the homeless as 'wandering abroad and lodging in any barn or outhouse, or in any deserted or unoccupied building . . . not having a visible means of subsistence and not giving a good account of oneself' has now been repealed. Despite its limitations, the Housing Act, 1988 is certainly a welcome development; whether or not it will be interpreted in such a manner as to substantially improve the lot of the homeless 'losers' remains to be seen.

Research has shown that there is a fundamental relationship between poverty and homelessness. In Ireland the majority of those who make up the 'long-term homeless' come from backgrounds characterised by grinding poverty. Many of them have also suffered severe emotional deprivation. And poverty is on the increase in Ireland, which inevitably means that the number of potentially homeless people is also on the increase. But poverty does not just happen; it is caused and perpetuated by the economic, legal, educational, medical and welfare structures in our society. It must therefore be possible to take steps to combat poverty at a structural level. To what extent have such steps been taken over the last decade? A study published by the Institute of Public Administration in 1982 states:

> As a response to poverty, social policy has to some extent improved the conditions of life for the poor and disadvantaged in Ireland. It has not, however, made any real impact on the overall pattern of social inequality – in some cases it has even perpetuated and accentuated existing inequalities. The reduction of inequality has never actually been set down as a goal for social policy however. It is a characteristic of liberal democracies such as Ireland that social policy is not spelt out clearly *since it is always potentially controversial*. [Italics mine.] This absence of a coherent social policy, however, means that there are no clear objectives and that there is a lack of co-ordination in, and control over, social policy. In Ireland this situation is exacerbated by the absence of data and of research studies on the outcomes of social policy . . .
>
> (*Poverty and Social Policy*, Joyce, L. and McCashin, A., Dublin, 1982, pp. 111, 112)

Can we, the politicians, the trade unionists, the Church people, the public servants, the ordinary voting citizens – can we meet the challenge as we move into the final decade of the twentieth century of putting ourselves fully behind a social policy which is unequivocally geared towards combating poverty and eliminating the structural injustices which cause it? This *is* a controversial question, but it is the only one worth asking. We get, as the old saying goes, the leaders and politicians we deserve. Recent research suggests that the Irish people are steadily losing faith in their leaders – but do we know clearly who we want in their places? Do we want leaders who will genuinely challenge the inequality in Irish society? I hope we do. I believe with Ghandi that 'there is enough in this world for everyone's need but there is not enough for everyone's greed.' There is enough in Ireland for all of us, the real problem lies in the way in which our wealth is distributed.

APPENDIX 1

AMENDED COPY OF THE BASIC FOUNDING PRINCIPLES AND FOUNDING PHILOSOPHY OF THE IRISH SIMON COMMUNITIES

This Philosophy and Principles being:—

1. Simon came into existence to work with the homeless and rootless, socially isolated, socially handicapped, unemployable men, women, children and groups.
2. Simon is a Way of Life — an alternative for people who cannot function adequately in everyday society: a Movement of Concern committed to being both a 'venture in Care' and an alerting body.
3. Simon is a democratic group based structure.
4. Simon groups, projects, complexes and Communities are structured on the creative leadership system with feedback and communication at all levels.
5. Simon Communities are the 'caring and cared with' living, working and re-creating co-equally.
6. Simon aims not to undertake single sex work, except in very special circumstances. The community comprises men and women couples and families and . . . .
(*Community* meaning the whole Simon complex).
7. Simon aims to run non-selective open houses of hospitality, shelters, cafés, and other experimental units, based on the four-tier structure covering all breakdown patterns within the framework of the homeless and rootless. It seeks not to specialise, except in exceptional circumstances.

8. Simon is primarily committed to the longterm care and containment of the homeless, rootless, and unemployable, and does not overtly aim for 'rehabilitation', nevertheless maintains emergency, short-term centres, offering social workers necessary facilities and providing opportunities for assessing the needs of those residents in a catchment area.
9. Simon avoids the use of the term 'hostel'.
10. Simon will not part a resident and his/her animal.
11. Simon seeks never to duplicate work which any other body would and could do more effectively. Simon comes in where others leave off, to meet the need where the need is greatest.
12. One community alone can never be Simon: Simon is a complex and a circuit.

There is nothing new about Simon: Simon is an amalgam of many experiments including those of Dorothy Day, Abbé Pierre, Mario Borelli, Maxwell Jones, Bram Peake and Tom Dooley, developing techniques and a methodology of its own.

Simon is committed to working from the bottom.

Simon is committed to the establishment of a caring society.

APPENDIX 2

STATISTICS ON HOMELESS PEOPLE IN DUBLIN CITY FROM SURVEY CARRIED OUT BY DUBLIN SIMON COMMUNITY, SEPTEMBER 1981 – JUNE 1983

		TOTAL NUMBER	:	**98**
Sex	:	Male	:	82
	:	Female	:	16
Marital Status	:	Married	:	6
	:	Single	:	62
	:	Separated	:	16
	:	Not Available	:	14
Origin	:	Dublin	:	48
	:	Country	:	39
	:	Not Available	:	11
Time Out	:	Less than 6 months	:	12
	:	6-12 months	:	28
	:	More than 12 months	:	57
	:	Not Available	:	1
Movements	:	Stationary	:	80
	:	Seasonal	:	11
	:	Not Available	:	7
Source of Income	:	Assistance	:	59
	:	D.P.M.A.	:	13
	:	Other	:	9
	:	Not Available	:	17
Institutions	:	Orphanage	:	11
	:	Juvenile Detention/Prison	:	60
Type of Offence	:	Minor	:	56
	:	Serious	:	4
Hospitals	:	General – short term	:	42
		– long term	:	2
	:	Psychiatric – short term	:	30
		– long term	:	2

Drinking Patterns	:	Problems	:	35
	:	Regular	:	31
	:	Not Available	:	32
Drugs	:	Prescribed Medication	:	23
	:	Illicit	:	31
	:	Not Available	:	44
Former Employment	:	Occasional	:	42
	:	Regular	:	4
	:	Skilled	:	6
	:	Unskilled	:	40
	:	Never Worked	:	11
Hostels	:	Occasional	:	50
	:	Never	:	38
	:	Not Available	:	10

14 – 18 YEARS **Females 7; Males 4**

Marital Status	:	Single	:	11
Origin	:	Dublin	:	11
Time Out	:	Less than 6 months	:	2
	:	6-12 months	:	6
	:	More than 12 months	:	3
Movements	:	Seasonal	:	–
	:	Stationary	:	11
Source of Income	:	Other	:	5
	:	Not Available	:	6
Institutions	:	Orphanage	:	1
	:	Juvenile Detention	:	4
Type of Offence	:	Minor	:	4
Hospital	:	General – short term	:	6
	:	Psychiatric – short term	:	2
Drinking Patterns	:	Regular	:	3
	:	Not Available	:	8
Drugs	:	Illicit	:	6
	:	Not Available	:	5
Employment	:	All unemployed – never worked		
Hostels	:	Occasional	:	5
	:	Never	:	4
	:	Not Available	:	2
Reasons Out	:	Strict Rules;		
	:	Cannot Settle;		
	:	Thrown out by families		

18 – 40 YEARS			**Females 3; Males 47**	
Origin	: Dublin	:	1	26
	: Country	:	2	18
	: Not Available	:	–	3
Status	: Married	:	1	16
	: Single	:	2	10
	: Separated	:	–	10
	: Not Available	:	–	11
Time Out	: Less than 6 months	:	2	4
	: 6-12 months	:	–	13
	: More than 12 months	:	1	30
Movements	: Stationary	:	2	36
	: Seasonal	:	1	7
	: Not Available	:	–	4
Source of Income	: Assistance	:	3	34
	: D.P.M.A.	:	–	7
	: Other	:	–	–
	: Not Available	:	–	6
Institutions	: Orphanage	:	–	4
	: Juvenile Detention	:	–	–
	: Prison	:	–	39
Type of Offence	: Minor	:	–	35
	: Serious	:	–	4
Hospital	: General – short term	:	2	20
	– long term	:	–	2
	: Psychiatric – short term	:	–	13
	– long term	:	–	1
Drinking Patterns	: Problem	:	1	16
	: Regular	:	2	12
	: Not Available	:	–	19
Drugs	: Prescribed medication	:	1	11
	: Illicit Drugs	:	–	21
	: Not Available	:	2	15
Former Employment	: Occasional	:	1	28
	: Regular	:	–	–
	: Skilled	:	–	2
	: Unskilled	:	1	26
Hostels	: Occasional	:	1	31
	: Never	:	2	11
	: Not Available	:	–	5
Reasons offered for not being in Shelter	: Rules too strict in hostels; barred from hostels; won't bother; hostels too violent; cannot cope.			

40 YEARS ±			**Females 6;**	**Males 31**
Origin	:	Dublin :	–	10
	:	Country :	3	16
	:	Not Available :	3	5
Status	:	Married :	1	4
	:	Single :	4	19
	:	Separated :	–	6
	:	Not Available :	1	2
Time Out	:	Less than 6 months :	–	4
	:	6-12 months :	1	8
	:	More than 12 months :	4	19
	:	Not Available :	1	–
Movements	:	Stationary :	4	27
	:	Seasonal :	–	3
	:	Not Available :	2	1
Source of Income	:	Assistance :	2	20
	:	D.P.M.A. :	1	5
	:	Other :	–	4
	:	Not Available :	3	2
Institution	:	Orphanage :	–	6
	:	Juvenile Detention/ Prison :	3	14
Type of Offence	:	Minor :	3	14
	:	Serious :	–	–
Hospitals	:	General – short term :	4	10
		– long term :	–	–
	:	Psychiatric – short term :	2	13
		– long term :	–	1
Drinking Patterns	:	Problem :	3	15
	:	Regular :	2	12
	:	Not Available :	1	4
Drugs	:	Prescribed Medication :	3	8
	:	Illicit Drugs :	1	3
	:	Not Available :	2	20
Former Employment	:	Occasional :	2	11
	:	Regular :	1	3
	:	Skilled :	1	3
	:	Unskilled :	2	11
Hostels	:	Occasional :	1	12
	:	Never :	3	18
	:	Not Available :	2	1

Reasons offered for not being in Shelter	:	Rules and regulations too strict; fear of hostels; prefer to stay out; pressure in hostels too much; fear of overcrowding in hostels; personality problems; financial problems.